UNPLUGGED!

A Practical Guide to Managing

Teenage Stress in the Digital Age

Proven Techniques for Promoting Emotional Wellness, Achieving Healthy Habits, and Building Resilience

I0106299

Oreste J. DAversa, CPC

Life Coach

PUBLISHER'S NOTE

This book is designed to provide accurate and authoritative information. information in regard to the subject matter covered. It is sold with the understanding that neither the author nor publisher is engaged in rendering psychological, legal, or other professional service. If psychological, legal, professional advice or other expert assistance is required, the services of a professional in that field should be sought. The principles and concepts presented in this book are the opinions of the author and are based on his interpretations of the aforementioned principles. Neither the author nor publisher is liable or responsible to any person or entity for any errors contained on this book, or website, or for any special, incidental, or consequential damage caused or alleged to be caused directly or indirectly by the information contained on this book or website. Any application of the techniques, ideas, and suggestions in this book is at the reader's sole discretion and risk.

No part of this publication may be reproduced, redistributed, taught, stored in a retrieval system, or transmitted, in any form, or by any means, electronic, mechanical, photocopy, recording, or otherwise, without the prior written permission of the publisher.

FIRST EDITION

ISBN: 978-1-952294-22-8

Library of Congress Control Number: 2023910091

Published by: Cutting Edge Technology Publishing

TABLE OF CONTENTS

THIS

PAGE

INTENTIONALLY

LEFT

BLANK

About The Author

Oreste J. DAversa, (O-rest-ee DA-versa) CPC
(Certified Professional Coach) is a Life Coach, Career/Job Search
Coach, and College Major Coach
(**www.CollegeMajorCoaching.com**).
He is the owner of Metropolitan Small Business Coaching LLC
(**www.MetroSmallBusinessCoaching.com**)
as a Business Coach, Consultant, and Trainer.

Mr. D'Aversa is also an Adjunct Faculty member as a
University Lecturer at **CUNY – Fashion Institute of Technology
(FIT)** in New York City.

He is an Inter-Faith (All-Faiths) Minister
(**www.GodLovesYouAndMe.org**) ordained by
The New Seminary in New York City, New York.

He appears on podcasts, radio, and television discussing his
expertise in business-related and personal growth subjects.

He is the author of the following books:

- **Life Beyond the Pandemic: A Practical New Journey
Handbook**

- **The Resume and Cover Letter Writing Toolkit for the
Successful Job Seeker**

- **Power Interviewing: Proven Job Interview Techniques That
Get You Results!**

- The Step-by-Step Business Networking Kit: The Ultimate Business Networking System that Delivers Superior Results!

- SELL More Technology NOW!

- Selling for Non-Selling Professionals©

- Baby Boomer Entrepreneur: Implementing the Boomer Business Success System ®: The Complete and Proven Guide to Starting a Successful Business, having Financial Freedom with the Lifestyle that You Want

- Discovering Your Life Purpose: The Journey Within - The True Guide to Achieving Unlimited Happiness, Prosperity and Personal Fulfillment

- The Seven Simple Principles of Prosperity: Practical Exercises to Achieve a Rich, Happy and Joyous Life

- I Didn't Get a Chance to Say Good-bye ... Now What Can I Do?

- Write Your Own Funeral Service

- Healing the Holes in My Soul!: How I Saved My Own Life, Became Whole to Lead a Happy, Fulfilling and Joyous Life!

Acknowledgments

To the Teenagers and Parents,

As I reflect on the completion of **"Unplugged! A Practical Guide to Managing Teenage Stress in the Digital Age,"** I am filled with gratitude and admiration for the incredible journey we have embarked upon together. This book has been written to improve the lives of teenagers (and their parents) in the digital age.

To the teenagers, this book is a testament to your resilience, strength, and unwavering spirit. I applaud your willingness to confront the unique challenges posed by the digital world head-on. You have demonstrated a remarkable capacity for growth, adaptability, and self-reflection. It is my sincere hope that the strategies and techniques presented in this book empower you to navigate the complexities of modern-day life with confidence, emotional wellness, and a sense of purpose.

To the parents, I extend my deepest gratitude for your commitment to the well-being of your teenagers. Your love, guidance, and unwavering support are invaluable. I acknowledge the profound responsibility you bear in navigating the uncharted waters of parenting in the digital age. Your dedication to fostering open communication, setting healthy boundaries, and modeling positive digital habits is commendable. This book aims to serve as a resource and companion on this transformative journey, providing you with insights, strategies, and practical tools to support your teenagers in building resilience and achieving emotional wellness.

I also wish to express my appreciation to the professionals and experts who have contributed their knowledge, research, and insights to this project. Your expertise and passion for promoting the well-being of teenagers have been instrumental in shaping this guidebook. It is through your collective efforts that we have been able to compile a comprehensive and practical resource that addresses the multifaceted challenges faced by teenagers in the digital age.

I also would like to acknowledge the following vendors for the use of their images: Designed by Freepik (Freepik.com) and Pixabay.com.

Finally, I extend my heartfelt gratitude to the readers who have entrusted me with their time and attention. It is my sincerest hope that "Unplugged!" serves as a source of inspiration, guidance, and empowerment for both teenagers and parents alike. May this book be a catalyst for meaningful conversations, positive change, and a renewed sense of purpose in managing teenage stress and embracing the joys and opportunities that the digital age offers.

Preface

In the bustling world, we inhabit today, modern-day life has evolved into a complex and intricate tapestry, presenting challenges and opportunities like never before. Amidst this intricacy, one group that finds themselves navigating an especially demanding landscape is teenagers. The advent of the digital age has transformed the very fabric of their existence, offering incredible connectivity, but also exposing them to a myriad of stressors that previous generations never had to contend with.

"Unplugged! A Practical Guide to Managing Teenage Stress in the Digital Age" is a book that seeks to address this pressing issue head-on. Its primary aim is to equip teenagers, their parents, and the wider community with proven techniques for promoting emotional wellness, achieving healthy habits, and building resilience in an era dominated by the relentless influx of digital technology.

This guidebook is born out of a recognition that the challenges faced by today's teenagers are unparalleled. The use of smartphones, social media, and instant communication has revolutionized the way they interact, learn, and perceive the world. However, this constant connectivity comes at a cost, as the digital realm has infiltrated every aspect of their lives, blurring the boundaries between the virtual and the real.

In "Unplugged!", we acknowledge the significant impact this digital saturation has on teenage stress levels. Adolescence is already a time of immense change and self-discovery, where hormonal fluctuations, academic pressures, and social dynamics intertwine to create a uniquely intense experience. Add to this the constant influx of information, the fear of missing out, and the pressure to conform to idealized online personas, and it becomes evident why teenage stress levels are reaching alarming heights.

Through this book, I aim to provide practical strategies to help teenagers navigate the digital age with resilience and emotional well-being intact. I firmly believe that by fostering healthy habits and promoting a balanced approach to technology, teenagers can harness its benefits without succumbing to its pitfalls. By encouraging regular unplugged breaks, fostering meaningful relationships, cultivating mindfulness, and developing effective stress-management techniques, teenagers can regain control over their lives and thrive in this ever-evolving world.

"Unplugged!" also recognizes the vital role parents, educators, and mentors play in supporting teenagers on this journey. This book serves as a resource for adults seeking a deeper understanding of the challenges faced by today's youth and provides practical guidance on fostering open communication, setting healthy boundaries, and modeling positive digital habits.

Throughout these pages, readers will find a wealth of research-backed information, and expert insights that demonstrate the transformative power of managing teenage stress in the digital age. From creating technology-free zones to engaging in physical activities, from developing healthy sleep patterns to fostering meaningful connections, each chapter offers practical techniques that can be implemented in everyday life.

Ultimately, **"Unplugged! A Practical Guide to Managing Teenage Stress in the Digital Age"** aims to empower teenagers, their families, and their communities to navigate the complexities of modern-day life with confidence, resilience, and emotional well-being. By embracing a balanced approach to technology and equipping oneself with proven techniques, it is my belief that teenagers can transcend the challenges of the digital age and embrace the fullness of their potential.

May this book serve as a guiding light, helping teenagers and their support networks forge a path toward a healthier, happier, and more fulfilling existence in an increasingly interconnected world.

NOTES

Introduction

Welcome to **"Unplugged! A Practical Guide to Managing Teenage Stress in the Digital Age."** We want nothing more than to see our teenagers flourish and thrive in today's fast-paced and technology-driven world. However, we also recognize the unique challenges they face when it comes to managing stress, navigating academic pressures, handling peer influences, combating bullying, engaging with social media, understanding the political climate, and healing from trauma. That's why I have created this comprehensive guide to equip both your teenager and their parents with proven techniques for promoting emotional wellness, achieving healthy habits, and building resilience.

In **Chapter 1: <u>Stress</u> - Managing Stress in the Teenage Years and Beyond**, I delve into the power of mindfulness and self-reflection. Through practices such as meditation, journaling, and walking in nature, teenagers will discover effective tools to manage stress, cultivate inner calm, and find balance amidst the chaos of everyday life.

Chapter 2: <u>Academic Pressures</u> - Finding Balance: Managing Schoolwork and Personal Life, focuses on empowering teenagers to thrive academically while maintaining a healthy personal life. They will learn essential skills such as time management, study techniques, and self-care strategies to optimize their productivity, enhance their learning experience, and prevent burnout.

In **Chapter 3: <u>Peer Pressure</u> - Navigating Healthy Relationships and Building Resilience**. Teenagers will gain invaluable insights into cultivating positive self-talk, finding strength in peer support, and embracing the transformative power of community service. These skills will empower them to make healthy choices, foster strong relationships, and develop resilience in the face of peer pressures and societal expectations.

In **Chapter 4: <u>Bullying</u> - Recognizing and Addressing Bullying: Empowering Individuals to Take Action,** we tackle the sensitive issue of bullying head-on. Your teenager will learn strategies to build self-esteem, resolve conflicts peacefully, and acquire social skills that promote respect and empathy. By empowering them to stand up against bullying, we aim to create a safe and inclusive environment for all.

The impact of social media on teenage well-being cannot be overlooked, and that's why **Chapter 5: <u>Social Media</u>: Navigating the Digital Landscape for Healthy Engagement and Well-being** is crucial. Your teenager will explore the importance of setting boundaries, practicing mindful social media use, and managing their digital footprint. By mastering these skills, they can maintain a healthy relationship with technology and prioritize their well-being in the digital world.

Chapter 6: <u>Political Climate</u>: Finding Common Ground: Building Bridges in a Divided Political Climate helps your teenager navigate the complexities of the political landscape. By providing diverse perspectives, promoting media literacy, and fostering open-mindedness, they will learn to engage in constructive conversations, embrace empathy, and bridge divides in a polarized society.

Lastly, **Chapter 7: <u>Trauma</u> - Understanding the Impact of Trauma: Building a Foundation for Recovery** acknowledges the profound effect of trauma on your teenager's well-being. We emphasize the importance of professional counseling, creative expression, and physical exercise as essential components of the healing journey. By equipping your teenager with the resources to process trauma and build resilience, we support their path toward recovery and growth.

Throughout this book, you will find practical exercises, and evidence-based techniques that have been carefully curated to address the unique challenges faced by today's teenagers. I encourage you to read alongside your teenager, fostering open communication and shared growth. Together, let's empower our teenagers to navigate the complexities of the digital age, promote emotional well-being, achieve healthy habits, and build resilience.

NOTES

Chapter 1: <u>Stress</u>
Managing Stress in the Teenage Years and Beyond

In the tumultuous journey of adolescence and the transition into adulthood, stress becomes a constant companion. From the pressures of academic performance to the complexities of social interactions, the teenage years can often feel like a rollercoaster ride. In this chapter, I delve into the art of managing stress and explore powerful techniques that can help teenagers not only navigate the challenges they face but also cultivate emotional well-being that extends far beyond their teenage years. Through the practice of meditation, the cathartic power of journaling, and the positive effects of immersing oneself in nature, I unveil a toolkit for stress management that empowers teenagers to build resilience, find inner calm, and thrive amidst the demands of the digital age. Let us embark on a transformative journey that will enable teenagers to conquer stress, embrace emotional wellness, and lay a foundation for a fulfilling future.

SECTION A: MEDITATION - CULTIVATING INNER CALM IN THE DIGITAL AGE

In today's fast-paced and constantly connected digital world, teenagers are facing unprecedented levels of stress and anxiety. The pressures of academics, social dynamics, and the constant bombardment of information through technology can leave them feeling overwhelmed and mentally exhausted. In this section, I explore the practice of meditation as a powerful tool for managing stress, cultivating emotional well-being, and finding inner calm amidst the chaos of the digital age.

Understanding Meditation

Meditation is an ancient practice that involves focusing one's attention and achieving a state of mental clarity and emotional balance. It offers a respite from external noise and distractions, allowing individuals to turn inward and connect with their inner selves. By training the mind to be present in the moment, meditation can bring a sense of calm, clarity, and perspective.

Benefits of Meditation for Teenagers:

Meditation holds numerous benefits for teenagers in managing stress and promoting emotional well-being:

a. Stress Reduction: Regular meditation practice has been shown to reduce stress hormones, lower anxiety levels, and improve overall emotional resilience. It provides teenagers with a valuable tool to navigate the challenges they face daily.

b. Improved Concentration: Meditation helps teenagers develop the ability to focus their attention and sustain concentration. This skill becomes particularly beneficial during academic pursuits and studying.

c. Emotional Regulation: By cultivating mindfulness and self-awareness, meditation empowers teenagers to observe their thoughts and emotions without judgment. This awareness allows them to respond to challenging situations with greater clarity and emotional control.

d. Enhanced Self-Reflection: Meditation encourages self-reflection, fostering a deeper understanding of one's own thoughts, beliefs, and values. This introspection aids teenagers in developing a strong sense of self and making informed decisions aligned with their personal growth.

Getting Started with Meditation:

a. Creating a Quiet Space: Designating a quiet and peaceful space for meditation can help teenagers establish a conducive environment for practice. It could be a comfortable corner in their room or any other area where they feel relaxed and undisturbed.

b. Choosing a Technique: There are various meditation techniques to explore, such as focused breathing, body scan, loving-kindness meditation, or guided visualization. Teenagers can experiment with different techniques to find the one that resonates with them the most.

A sample meditation that I have personally created is available free of charge on YouTube and is called - **Learn a Basic Meditation: 1-2-3-4 Technique - Oreste J. DAversa** (https://youtu.be/ogO_LeUA7-I)

c. Setting Realistic Goals: Starting with short meditation sessions of 5 minutes and gradually increasing the duration can make the practice more accessible and sustainable. It is essential for teenagers to set realistic goals that fit their schedule and allow for consistency.

d. Cultivating Consistency: Consistency is key to reaping the benefits of meditation. Encouraging teenagers to establish a regular practice by incorporating it into their daily routine can help them make it a habit.

Integrating Meditation into Daily Life:

a. Mindful Moments: Encouraging teenagers to incorporate moments of mindfulness throughout their day can be as simple as taking a few conscious breaths before starting a task or pausing to observe their surroundings during a walk. These small moments of mindfulness reinforce the benefits of meditation in everyday life.

b. Mindful Technology Use: In the digital age, technology often becomes a source of stress and distraction. Teaching teenagers to use technology mindfully by setting boundaries, taking breaks, and being aware of its impact on their well-being can help create a healthier relationship with technology.

c. Mindful Relationships: Meditation can enhance interpersonal relationships by promoting empathy, active listening, and compassionate communication. Encouraging teenagers to approach their interactions with friends, family, and peers from a place of mindfulness can foster healthier and more meaningful connections.

In the digital age, where constant connectivity and information overload contribute to heightened stress levels among teenagers, meditation provides a powerful antidote. By cultivating mindfulness and inner calm, teenagers can navigate the challenges of the digital age with greater resilience and emotional well-being. The practice of meditation offers a sanctuary amidst the chaos, allowing teenagers to find moments of stillness and self-reflection. It equips them with the tools to manage stress, improve concentration, regulate emotions, and foster a deeper connection with themselves and others.

As teenagers embark on their journey of managing stress in the digital age, it is essential to remember that meditation is a personal practice. Each individual may resonate with different techniques and approaches. It is a journey of self-discovery, where teenagers can explore various meditation practices and find what works best for them.

Integrating meditation into daily life goes beyond the practice itself. It involves creating mindful moments, setting boundaries with technology, and fostering meaningful connections with others. By incorporating mindfulness into their routines, teenagers can experience the transformative power of meditation throughout their lives.

This book invites teenagers to embrace the practice of meditation as a means to cultivate emotional wellness, achieve healthy habits, and build resilience. It empowers them to step away from the digital noise, finds their inner calm, and thrive in the face of the challenges that lie ahead.

Through the practice of meditation, teenagers can discover a powerful tool for self-care and personal growth. As they navigate the complexities of the digital age, meditation becomes a guiding light, providing them with the clarity and peace needed to navigate the storms of life. By incorporating meditation into their lives, teenagers can unlock their full potential, cultivate emotional well-being, and build a foundation for a balanced and fulfilling future.

Embark on this journey of self-discovery and embrace the transformative power of meditation. Find solace in the present moment, connect with your inner self, and unleash the resilience and strength that lies within. The path to managing teenage stress in the digital age starts with a single breath, a moment of stillness, and a commitment to your well-being. Let meditation be your companion on this transformative journey.

SECTION B: JOURNALING - UNLOCKING EMOTIONAL EXPRESSION AND SELF-DISCOVERY

In the digital age, where the pace of life is fast and distractions abound, teenagers often struggle to find ways to express their thoughts and emotions authentically. Journaling offers a transformative practice that allows them to navigate the complexities of teenage years, manage stress, and foster emotional well-being. In this section, we explore the power of journaling as a tool for self-reflection, emotional expression, and self-discovery.

The Art of Journaling

Journaling is the act of putting pen to paper and capturing one's thoughts, feelings, and experiences in a personal journal. It provides a safe and private space for teenagers to explore their inner world, reflect on their experiences, and make sense of their emotions. Whether through traditional handwritten journals or digital platforms, journaling offers a powerful means of self-expression and self-discovery.

Benefits of Journaling for Teenagers

Engaging in regular journaling practice brings numerous benefits to teenagers in managing stress and promoting emotional well-being:

a. Emotional Release: Journaling provides a healthy outlet for teenagers to express their emotions, frustrations, and fears. By putting their thoughts and feelings into words, they can gain a sense of release and relief.

b. Self-Reflection: Journaling encourages introspection and self-awareness. It allows teenagers to explore their values, beliefs, and aspirations, leading to a deeper understanding of themselves.

c. Problem-Solving: Writing about challenges and dilemmas can help teenagers gain clarity and perspective. Journaling enables them to explore different solutions, evaluate options, and make informed decisions.

d. Stress Reduction: The act of journaling itself can be cathartic, helping teenagers process stress and anxiety. By externalizing their thoughts and concerns onto paper, they can experience a sense of relief and relaxation.

Getting Started with Journaling

a. Choose a Journal: Encourage teenagers to select a journal that resonates with them, whether it's a blank notebook, a guided journal with prompts, or a digital journaling app. The journal should feel inviting and safe for self-expression.

b. Set Aside Regular Time: Establishing a routine for journaling is crucial. Encourage teenagers to allocate dedicated time each day or week to engage in journaling. Consistency allows them to reap the full benefits of this practice.

c. Write Freely: Emphasize that there are no right or wrong ways to journal. Encourage teenagers to write freely, without judgment or concern for grammar or spelling. Remind them that the journal is for their eyes only, providing a space free from external scrutiny.

d. Explore Different Prompts: Journaling prompts can spark creativity and self-reflection. Encourage teenagers to experiment with prompts such as gratitude lists, personal affirmations, or reflections on specific experiences or challenges they face.

Integrating Journaling into Daily Life:

a. Emotional Check-Ins: Encourage teenagers to use journaling as a tool for emotional check-ins. They can write about their emotions, what triggers them, and explore strategies for emotional regulation.

b. Goal Setting and Tracking: Journaling can help teenagers set and track their goals. They can write about their aspirations, break them down into actionable steps, and reflect on progress over time.

c. Self-Care Reflections: Encourage teenagers to use journaling as a space to reflect on their self-care practices. They can write about activities that bring them joy, strategies for managing stress, and explore ways to prioritize their well-being.

d. Gratitude and Positive Reflections: Journaling about moments of gratitude and positive experiences can cultivate a positive mindset. Encourage teenagers to write about things they appreciate, accomplishments, or acts of kindness they've witnessed or received.

Journaling serves as a powerful tool for teenagers to navigate the challenges of the digital age, manage stress, and foster emotional well-being. By engaging in regular journaling practice, teenagers can unlock the benefits of emotional release, self-reflection, problem-solving, and stress reduction. Journaling provides a safe and private space for them to express their thoughts, feelings, and experiences, leading to greater self-awareness and personal growth.

As teenagers embark on their journaling journey, it is important to remember that there are no rules or limitations. Each journal entry is a unique expression of their inner world, and they have the freedom to explore their thoughts and emotions authentically. Journaling is a personal practice that can be adapted to individual preferences and needs.

Integrating journaling into daily life goes beyond the act of writing. It involves creating a routine, setting aside dedicated time for reflection, and exploring different prompts and techniques. Journaling can be incorporated into various aspects of teenagers' lives, such as emotional check-ins, goal setting, self-care reflections, and gratitude practices.

This guide invites teenagers to embrace journaling as a powerful tool for self-discovery, emotional well-being, and personal growth. It empowers them to engage in self-reflection, express their thoughts and emotions authentically, and navigate the complexities of teenage years with resilience.

In the journey of managing teenage stress in the digital age, journaling becomes a trusted companion, providing a space for teenagers to unload their burdens, gain clarity, and nurture their inner world. Through journaling, they can cultivate emotional wellness, achieve healthy habits, and build resilience that will support them throughout their lives.

Embark on this transformative journey of journaling and unlock the power of self-expression, self-discovery, and emotional well-being. Discover the therapeutic benefits of putting pen to paper, and let your journal be a sacred space for reflection, growth, and personal empowerment. By embracing journaling, teenagers can thrive in the digital age and nurture their emotional wellness, paving the way for a fulfilling and balanced future.

Remember, your journal holds the key to your inner world. Take this opportunity to explore, reflect, and cultivate a deeper understanding of yourself. Let your journal be your confidant, companion, and guide as you navigate the challenges and joys of the teenage years and beyond.

SECTION C: WALKING IN NATURE - CONNECTING WITH THE HEALING POWER OF THE OUTDOORS

In the hustle and bustle of the digital age, teenagers often find themselves immersed in a fast-paced and technology-driven world. The constant exposure to screens and digital devices can lead to feelings of overwhelm, stress, and disconnection. In this section, we explore the practice of walking in nature as a powerful tool for managing teenage stress, promoting emotional well-being, and fostering a deep connection with the natural world.

The Healing Power of Nature

Nature has long been recognized as a source of healing and rejuvenation. Walking in natural environments provides teenagers with an opportunity to disconnect from the digital world and reconnect with the beauty and serenity of the outdoors. Nature offers a calming and soothing effect on the mind and body, allowing for stress reduction and emotional restoration.

Benefits of Walking in Nature for Teenagers:
Engaging in regular walks in nature offers numerous benefits for teenagers in managing stress and promoting emotional well-being:

a. Stress Reduction: Walking in natural surroundings promotes relaxation, reduces stress hormones, and improves overall mood. It provides a reprieve from the demands and pressures of daily life.

b. Physical Well-being: Walking is a low-impact form of exercise that promotes cardiovascular health, improves fitness levels, and enhances overall physical well-being. The combination of fresh air, sunlight, and movement contributes to a healthy body and mind.

c. Cognitive Enhancement: Walking in nature has been shown to enhance cognitive function, including attention, memory, and creativity. The peacefulness of natural environments allows teenagers to clear their minds and improve focus and mental clarity.

d. Emotional Restoration: Nature has a profound impact on emotional well-being. Walking in natural settings can reduce symptoms of anxiety, and depression, and improve overall emotional resilience. It provides a space for reflection, introspection, and a sense of peace.

Tips for Walking in Nature:

a. Choose Natural Settings: Encourage teenagers to seek out natural settings for their walks, such as parks, forests, beaches, or trails. Being surrounded by greenery, bodies of water, and natural elements enhances the restorative effects of the experience.

b. Unplug from Technology: Encourage teenagers to disconnect from their digital devices during their nature walks. This allows them to fully immerse themselves in the present moment and experience the beauty of nature without distractions.

c. Mindful Walking: Guide teenagers to practice mindful walking during their nature walks. Encourage them to engage their senses, notice the sights, sounds, and smells of nature, and be fully present in the experience.

d. Set Intention: Encourage teenagers to set an intention for their nature walks, such as finding peace, seeking inspiration, or simply enjoying the beauty around them. Having a purpose can enhance the overall experience and foster a deeper connection with nature.

Incorporating Nature into Daily Life:

a. Daily Nature Breaks: Encourage teenagers to take short nature breaks throughout their day, even if it's just a few minutes spent in a nearby park or green space. These small doses of nature can have a positive impact on their well-being and help them recharge.

b. Nature-Based Activities: Suggest engaging in nature-based activities such as bird-watching, nature photography, or nature journaling. These activities deepen the connection with the natural world and provide opportunities for creativity and self-expression.

c. Environmental Awareness: Promote environmental awareness and stewardship by encouraging teenagers to learn about local ecosystems, participate in conservation efforts, or engage in volunteer work related to nature preservation.

Walking in nature offers teenagers a respite from the fast-paced digital world, allowing them to reconnect with themselves and the natural environment. By engaging in this simple yet powerful practice, teenagers can experience the physical, mental, and emotional benefits of walking in nature. Through the healing power of nature, teenagers can find solace, rejuvenation, and a sense of connection that is often missing in the digital age.

Walking in nature is not just a physical activity; it is an opportunity for teenagers to nourish their overall well-being. It provides a space for reflection, self-discovery, and a deeper understanding of themselves and the world around them. By immersing themselves in the beauty and serenity of natural environments, teenagers can find peace, clarity, and a renewed sense of vitality.

As we all navigate the challenges of the digital age, it is essential to prioritize our connection with nature. Encouraging teenagers to incorporate walks in nature into their daily lives can have a profound impact on their stress levels, emotional well-being, and overall quality of life. It allows them to step away from the constant stimulation of screens, engage their senses, and appreciate the wonders of the natural world.

"Unplugged: A Practical Guide to Managing Teenage Stress in the Digital Age," I invite teenagers to embrace the practice of walking in nature as a means to manage stress, cultivate emotional wellness, and foster a deep connection with the world around them. I encourage them to carve out time for regular walks, choose natural settings, and embrace the beauty and tranquility that nature offers.

By integrating the practice of walking in nature into their lives, teenagers can find balance, resilience, and a renewed sense of purpose. It is an opportunity to slow down, breathe in the fresh air, and engage in self-care that goes beyond the digital realm. Walking in nature becomes a powerful tool for promoting emotional well-being, achieving healthy habits, and building resilience in the face of the challenges of the digital age.

So, let us embark on this journey of walking in nature together. Let us explore the paths less traveled, soak in the beauty of the natural world, and allow its healing embrace to restore our spirits. By immersing ourselves in the tranquility of nature, we can find the inner peace and strength to navigate the complexities of teenage life and thrive in the digital age.

Remember, nature is always there, waiting to welcome us with open arms. So, put on your walking shoes, step outside, and let the healing power of nature guide you on a path toward emotional wellness, healthy habits, and resilience. Embrace the beauty, find solace in the stillness, and let nature be your sanctuary in the bustling digital age.

Chapter 2: <u>Academic Pressures</u> Finding Balance – Managing Schoolwork and Personal Life

In the fast-paced and demanding academic environment, teenagers often find themselves juggling multiple responsibilities and facing immense pressure to excel in their studies. This chapter delves into the crucial aspects of managing academic pressures and finding a balance between schoolwork and personal life. We will explore three essential sections that provide valuable insights and practical strategies: time management, study techniques, and self-care. By mastering these key elements, teenagers can optimize their academic performance while maintaining their overall well-being and enjoyment of life. Let us embark on a journey of discovery and empowerment as we navigate the challenges of academic pressures together.

SECTION A: TIME MANAGEMENT - MAXIMIZING PRODUCTIVITY AND ACHIEVING BALANCE

In today's fast-paced digital age, time has become a precious commodity, particularly for teenagers who are faced with numerous academic demands, extracurricular activities, and personal commitments. Effectively managing time is a crucial skill that not only enhances productivity but also promotes a healthy balance between academic pursuits and personal well-being. In this section, we will delve into the importance of time management for teenagers and explore proven techniques to optimize their use of time, reduce stress, and achieve greater success in their academic endeavors.

Understanding the Value of Time

Time is an invaluable resource that should be utilized wisely. Teenagers often find themselves overwhelmed by a multitude of tasks, leading to procrastination, burnout, and subpar performance. By recognizing the value of time and its impact on their overall well-being, teenagers can develop a mindset that prioritizes effective time management.

Setting Clear Goals and Priorities

One of the fundamental principles of time management is setting clear goals and priorities. Teenagers need to identify their short-term and long-term goals, both academically and personally. By establishing clear priorities, they can allocate their time and energy to tasks that align with their goals, ensuring a sense of purpose and direction.

Creating a Structured Schedule

A well-structured schedule is the backbone of effective time management. Teenagers should develop a daily or weekly schedule that includes dedicated time slots for various activities, such as classes, study sessions, extracurricular activities, and leisure. This helps create a sense of routine, reduces procrastination, and enhances productivity.

Prioritizing Tasks and Managing Deadlines

Prioritizing tasks based on urgency and importance is crucial for efficient time management. Teenagers should learn to distinguish between essential and non-essential tasks, focusing on high-priority items first. Additionally, managing deadlines effectively by breaking tasks into smaller, manageable chunks can help reduce overwhelm and ensure timely completion.

Utilizing Time-Management Tools and Techniques

With the advent of technology, teenagers have access to various time-management tools and techniques that can aid in organizing tasks and maximizing productivity. From digital calendars and task management apps to **The Pomodoro Technique** (The Pomodoro Technique is a time management method based on 25-minute stretches of focused work broken by five-minute breaks. Longer breaks, typically 15 to 30 minutes, are taken after four consecutive work intervals. Each work interval is called a Pomodoro, the Italian word for tomato). and other time-blocking methods, these tools and techniques can assist teenagers in better managing their time.

Avoiding Time Wasters

Time wasters, such as excessive social media usage, aimless internet browsing, and unnecessary distractions, can significantly hamper productivity. Teenagers should learn to identify and minimize these time wasters, setting boundaries and adopting mindful practices to stay focused and make the most of their time.

Balancing Academic Demands and Personal Well-being

While academic success is important, it should not come at the expense of personal well-being. Teenagers need to strike a balance between their academic pursuits and self-care activities. Incorporating breaks, exercise, hobbies, and quality time with friends and family into their schedule promotes overall well-being and prevents burnout.

Effective time management is a vital skill for teenagers to navigate the academic pressures they face in the digital age. By understanding the value of time, setting clear goals, creating a structured schedule, prioritizing tasks, utilizing time-management tools, avoiding time wasters, and balancing academic demands with personal well-being, teenagers can enhance their productivity, reduce stress, and achieve a healthier and more balanced lifestyle. With the right strategies and mindset, they can master time management and thrive academically while also enjoying a fulfilling teenage experience.

SECTION B: STUDY TECHNIQUES

In today's academic landscape, effective study techniques are essential for teenagers to succeed in their educational pursuits. With the increasing demands of coursework and exams, it is crucial to equip students with strategies that optimize their learning and retention. This section of the book delves into various study techniques that empower teenagers to enhance their academic performance while maintaining a healthy balance in their lives. By implementing these proven strategies, students can cultivate effective study habits and achieve their full potential.

Active Reading

Active reading is a technique that promotes engagement and comprehension while reading. It involves being actively involved in the reading process through strategies such as highlighting key points, annotating the text, and asking questions to deepen understanding. Research has shown that active reading improves retention and critical thinking skills (Willis & Farmer, 2020). By encouraging teenagers to actively interact with the material they are studying, they can extract meaning, make connections, and retain information more effectively.

Mind Mapping

Mind mapping is a visual technique that helps students organize and connect ideas. It involves creating a diagram that branches out from a central concept, with related ideas and subtopics radiating from it. Mind maps stimulate creativity, enhance memory retention, and facilitate a holistic understanding of complex subjects (Buzan, 2010). By using colors, images, and keywords, teenagers can create visually appealing and meaningful mind maps that serve as powerful study aids.

Practice Testing

Practice testing involves actively retrieving information from memory through quizzes, flashcards, or self-testing. Research has consistently shown that practice testing improves long-term retention and enhances learning (Roediger & Butler, 2011). By regularly testing their knowledge and actively recalling information, teenagers reinforce their understanding and identify areas that require further review. Practice testing is a valuable tool for self-assessment and preparation for exams.

Time Management

Effective time management is crucial for academic success. It involves planning and prioritizing tasks, allocating dedicated study time, and avoiding procrastination. Research has shown that students who manage their time well experience less stress, achieve higher grades, and have better overall well-being (Britton & Tesser, 1991). By teaching teenagers strategies such as setting realistic goals, creating study schedules, and breaking tasks into manageable chunks, they can develop discipline and maximize their productivity.

Collaborative Learning

Collaborative learning involves working with peers in study groups or project teams to enhance understanding and knowledge sharing. By discussing concepts, explaining ideas to others, and engaging in group activities, teenagers can deepen their comprehension and develop critical thinking skills (Johnson et al., 2014). Collaborative learning fosters communication, cooperation, and mutual support, creating a positive and enriching study environment.

The study techniques explored in this section offer teenagers valuable tools to improve their learning outcomes and navigate the academic pressures they face. By implementing active reading, mind mapping, practice testing, and effective time management, students can enhance their study habits, retain information more effectively, and achieve academic success.

Furthermore, collaborative learning provides a supportive and interactive environment that promotes engagement and critical thinking. By incorporating these strategies into their study routine, teenagers can approach their academic responsibilities with confidence and develop lifelong skills that will benefit them in their educational journey and beyond.

SECTION C: SELF-CARE

Self-care is a crucial aspect of managing academic pressures and promoting overall well-being for teenagers. In today's fast-paced and demanding world, it is essential to prioritize self-care practices that help teenagers maintain balance, reduce stress, and enhance their emotional and physical health. This section explores various self-care strategies that teenagers can incorporate into their lives to support their academic journey and foster resilience. By taking care of themselves, teenagers can better cope with the challenges they face, maintain healthy habits, and build a foundation for long-term well-being.

One effective self-care strategy for teenagers is prioritizing sleep. Adequate sleep is essential for cognitive function, concentration, and overall health. Research has shown that sleep deprivation can negatively impact academic performance, attention span, and memory recall (Carskadon et al., 2006). Encouraging teenagers to establish a consistent sleep schedule, practice good sleep hygiene, and create a relaxing bedtime routine can significantly improve their sleep quality and overall well-being.

Physical Activity

Physical activity is another important component of self-care for teenagers. Engaging in regular exercise has numerous benefits, including reducing stress, improving mood, and boosting cognitive function. Exercise increases the production of endorphins, which are natural mood-enhancing chemicals in the brain. It also promotes better sleep, enhances concentration, and increases overall energy levels (Mandolesi et al., 2018). Encouraging teenagers to participate in activities they enjoy, such as sports, dancing, or hiking, can help them incorporate physical activity into their daily routine and experience positive effects on their well-being.

Mindfulness and Relaxation Techniques

Mindfulness and relaxation techniques are powerful tools for self-care and stress management. Teaching teenagers techniques such as deep breathing exercises, meditation, and mindfulness practices can help them develop greater self-awareness, reduce anxiety, and improve their ability to handle academic pressures.

Mindfulness-based interventions have been shown to reduce stress, enhance attention, and improve overall psychological well-being in teenagers (Dunning et al., 2019). Incorporating mindfulness exercises into daily routines or engaging in activities such as yoga or tai chi can provide teenagers with a sense of calm and balance amidst their academic demands.

Nutrition

Nutrition plays a vital role in supporting both physical and mental well-being. A balanced diet rich in nutrients is essential for optimal brain function, energy levels, and overall health. Encouraging teenagers to make healthy food choices, such as consuming fruits, vegetables, whole grains, and lean proteins, can provide them with the necessary nutrients to support their cognitive abilities and maintain stable energy levels throughout the day. Additionally, staying hydrated by drinking an adequate amount of water is crucial for maintaining focus and preventing fatigue.

Social Connections and Maintaining a Supportive Network

Lastly, fostering social connections and maintaining a supportive network is an important aspect of self-care for teenagers. Strong social relationships provide emotional support, a sense of belonging, and opportunities for growth and personal development. Encouraging teenagers to spend time with friends and family, participate in social activities, and seek support when needed can contribute to their overall well-being and resilience.

Self-care is a fundamental component of managing academic pressures and promoting well-being for teenagers. Prioritizing sleep, engaging in regular physical activity, practicing mindfulness, maintaining a balanced diet, and fostering social connections are all essential strategies for supporting teenagers' self-care journey. By incorporating these self-care practices into their lives, teenagers can enhance their ability to cope with academic challenges, maintain healthy habits, and cultivate resilience for a successful and balanced academic experience.

NOTES

Chapter 3: <u>Peer Pressure</u> Navigating Healthy Relationships and Building Self Resilience

In the journey of adolescence, peer pressure plays a significant role in shaping the experiences and choices of teenagers. It is crucial to equip them with the necessary tools to navigate the complexities of social interactions and develop resilience in the face of external influences. This chapter delves into the empowering techniques that can help teenagers effectively manage peer pressure and cultivate healthy relationships. We will explore the power of positive self-talk, the importance of peer support, and the transformative benefits of engaging in community service. By understanding these three key areas, teenagers can build a strong sense of self, establish meaningful connections, and contribute positively to their communities. Let's embark on this transformative journey of peer pressure management and resilience-building together.

SECTION A: POSITIVE SELF-TALK - EMPOWERING INNER DIALOGUE

In the realm of peer pressure, one of the most influential factors is the internal dialogue that takes place within a teenager's mind. Positive self-talk serves as a powerful tool to counteract negative external influences and cultivate a resilient mindset. By harnessing the power of affirmations, reframing thoughts, and nurturing self-belief, teenagers can develop a strong sense of self-worth and make choices aligned with their values and aspirations. This section explores the importance of positive self-talk in navigating peer pressure and building resilience. Let's delve into the techniques and strategies that can empower teenagers to embrace self-compassion, challenge limiting beliefs, and foster positive inner dialogue.

Understanding the Power of Self-Talk

Positive self-talk involves consciously shaping the thoughts and messages we tell ourselves. It influences our emotions, actions, and overall well-being. By recognizing the impact of self-talk, teenagers can gain control over their internal narrative and steer it towards positivity and self-empowerment.

Affirmations and Self-Compassion

Affirmations are powerful statements that reinforce positive qualities, beliefs, and intentions. They serve as a reminder of one's worth and potential, boosting self-confidence and resilience. Incorporating self-compassion into self-talk practices helps teenagers develop a kinder and more supportive relationship with themselves, fostering a sense of inner strength and acceptance.

Reframing Negative Thoughts

Peer pressure often triggers negative thoughts and self-doubt. Learning to reframe these thoughts can help teenagers challenge their validity and adopt a more optimistic perspective. By identifying cognitive distortions, questioning negative beliefs, and replacing them with more positive and realistic alternatives, teenagers can reshape their self-talk and build resilience against external pressures.

Cultivating a Growth Mindset

A growth mindset emphasizes the belief that abilities and intelligence can be developed through effort and perseverance. By adopting a growth mindset, teenagers can view challenges as opportunities for growth, embrace setbacks as learning experiences, and maintain a resilient attitude in the face of peer pressure. Encouraging a growth mindset through self-talk promotes resilience, adaptability, and a willingness to take on new challenges.

Harnessing Visualization and Self-Reflection

Visualization and self-reflection techniques can enhance the power of positive self-talk. By visualizing desired outcomes, teenagers can create a mental image of success and reinforce positive beliefs in their abilities. Self-reflection allows them to gain insights into their strengths, values, and goals, supporting a positive self-talk practice that aligns with their authentic selves.

Building Resilience Through Positive Affirmations

Positive affirmations tailored to specific challenges can bolster resilience in the face of peer pressure. By crafting affirmations that address self-esteem, assertiveness, and decision-making, teenagers can strengthen their ability to resist negative influences and make choices aligned with their values and well-being.

Positive self-talk is a powerful tool for navigating peer pressure and building resilience. By embracing affirmations, practicing self-compassion, reframing negative thoughts, cultivating a growth mindset, harnessing visualization and self-reflection, and using positive affirmations strategically, teenagers can foster a resilient inner dialogue that empowers them to navigate peer pressure and make choices that align with their emotional wellness and personal growth. By integrating positive self-talk practices into their lives, teenagers can develop the inner strength and resilience needed to thrive in the face of external influences.

Section B: Peer Support - Building Strong Connections and Resilient Relationships

Navigating the complex landscape of peer pressure requires a solid support system. Peer support plays a crucial role in helping teenagers manage the challenges they face and build resilience. By fostering healthy relationships, seeking guidance from trusted peers, and participating in supportive communities, teenagers can find comfort, encouragement, and guidance in their journey. This section explores the importance of peer support in navigating peer pressure and building resilience. Let's delve into the strategies and benefits of cultivating strong connections with peers.

The Power of Healthy Relationships

Healthy relationships provide a sense of belonging, understanding, and acceptance. They offer a safe space where teenagers can express their thoughts, share experiences, and receive support. Cultivating positive and supportive friendships helps teenagers counteract negative peer pressure, develop a sense of identity, and build resilience.

Identifying Trusted Peers

Seeking guidance from trusted peers is invaluable when facing peer pressure. Identifying individuals who share similar values, goals, and interests can create a network of support and understanding. Trusted peers can offer advice, perspective, and encouragement, providing a valuable source of reassurance and empowerment.

Peer Mentoring and Role Models

Peer mentoring programs and role models play a significant role in shaping teenagers' resilience. Mentors offer guidance, empathy, and wisdom based on their own experiences, helping teenagers navigate challenges and make informed decisions. By connecting with positive role models, teenagers gain inspiration and learn valuable life skills that contribute to their overall well-being.

Effective Communication and Assertiveness

Peer support fosters the development of effective communication and assertiveness skills. Teenagers learn to express their needs, boundaries, and opinions with confidence and respect. By honing these skills, they can navigate peer pressure situations, advocate for themselves, and make choices aligned with their values and well-being.

Building Supportive Communities

Engaging in supportive communities provides a broader network of peer support. These communities can include school clubs, extracurricular activities, online forums, and support groups. By participating in these communities, teenagers connect with like-minded individuals, share experiences, and gain access to valuable resources and guidance.

Peer Support in Challenging Times

Peer support becomes especially crucial during challenging times, such as during transitions, conflicts, or stressful events. Having a strong support system allows teenagers to lean on others for emotional support, advice, and encouragement. This support fosters resilience, helping teenagers navigate difficult situations and bounce back from adversity.

Peer support is a vital component of navigating peer pressure and building resilience in teenagers. By cultivating healthy relationships, seeking guidance from trusted peers, engaging in peer mentoring, developing effective communication and assertiveness skills, and participating in supportive communities, teenagers can access the benefits of peer support. These connections provide comfort, encouragement, and guidance in navigating peer pressure, making choices aligned with their values, and developing a resilient mindset. Peer support empowers teenagers to face challenges head-on, build resilience, and thrive in the midst of external influences.

SECTION C: COMMUNITY SERVICE - MAKING A DIFFERENCE AND BUILDING RESILIENCE

Community service offers teenagers a unique opportunity to make a positive impact on the world around them while simultaneously building their own resilience. Engaging in acts of service fosters empathy, compassion, and a sense of purpose, which are invaluable qualities for navigating peer pressure and developing a strong sense of self. This section explores the significance of community service in promoting emotional wellness, achieving healthy habits, and building resilience. Let's delve into the transformative power of community service and its benefits for teenagers.

Understanding the Importance of Community Service

Community service goes beyond fulfilling mandatory requirements; it is an opportunity to contribute to the betterment of society. Engaging in acts of service allows teenagers to develop a sense of empathy, expand their perspective, and understand the needs of others. By actively participating in community service, teenagers learn the value of giving back and become agents of positive change.

Building Empathy and Compassion

Community service cultivates empathy and compassion by exposing teenagers to diverse perspectives and experiences. Engaging in activities that support individuals or groups facing challenges fosters a deeper understanding of others' struggles and fosters a sense of connection. Developing empathy and compassion enables teenagers to navigate peer pressure with empathy and make choices that consider the well-being of themselves and others.

Developing a Sense of Purpose

Community service provides teenagers with a sense of purpose and meaning. Engaging in activities that align with their values and interests allows them to contribute to causes they care about. Having a sense of purpose empowers teenagers to resist negative peer pressure and make choices that align with their personal values and goals. It also enhances their self-esteem and sense of identity.

Enhancing Social Skills and Building Relationships

Community service offers opportunities for teenagers to interact with individuals from diverse backgrounds. Through collaboration and teamwork, they develop essential social skills, such as communication, problem-solving, and cooperation. Building relationships with fellow volunteers and the community strengthens their support network and provides a sense of belonging and connection.

Fostering Resilience through Challenges

Community service may present challenges, such as working in unfamiliar environments or facing obstacles in project implementation. Overcoming these challenges builds resilience in teenagers. It teaches them problem-solving, adaptability, and perseverance, skills that are essential for navigating the complexities of peer pressure and building a resilient mindset.

Cultivating Leadership and Civic Engagement

Engaging in community service allows teenagers to cultivate leadership skills and foster civic engagement. They have the opportunity to take initiative, organize projects, and mobilize others towards a common goal. By taking on leadership roles, teenagers develop confidence, responsibility, and a sense of agency, which are crucial for resisting negative peer pressure and making positive contributions to their communities.

Long-Term Impact and Personal Growth

The effects of community service extend beyond the immediate moment of engagement. Teenagers who actively participate in community service often experience personal growth and transformation. They develop a sense of civic responsibility, become advocates for social change, and carry the values of community service into their adult lives. Community service is a powerful tool for promoting emotional wellness, achieving healthy habits, and building resilience in teenagers. Engaging in acts of service fosters empathy, compassion, and a sense of purpose. It enhances social skills, cultivates leadership qualities, and fosters personal growth. Through community service, teenagers gain valuable experiences that help them navigate peer pressure, make choices aligned with their values, and contribute to the well-being of others. Embracing community service empowers teenagers to become positive agents of change and resilient individuals who are equipped to thrive in the face of challenges.

NOTES

Chapter 4: <u>Bullying</u> Recognizing and Addressing Bullying: Empowering Individuals to Take Action

In Chapter 04 of "Unplugged: A Practical Guide to Managing Teenage Stress in the Digital Age," we delve into the critical issue of bullying and its impact on the well-being of individuals. Bullying has become a pervasive problem in today's society, and it is crucial that we equip individuals with the necessary tools to recognize and address this issue effectively. This chapter focuses on three key areas: building self-esteem, conflict resolution, and social skills training. By exploring these topics, we aim to empower individuals to take action against bullying, promote a positive and inclusive environment, and cultivate resilience in the face of adversity. Together, let's work towards creating a safer and more supportive community for all.

SECTION A: BUILDING SELF-ESTEEM

In today's society, the impact of bullying on individuals, particularly teenagers, cannot be understated. One of the essential factors in combating bullying is building a strong sense of self-esteem. Adolescence is a critical period for developing self-worth and confidence, and it is crucial to equip young people with the tools to navigate these challenges effectively. In this section, we will explore the concept of self-esteem, its importance in countering bullying, and proven techniques for building and enhancing self-esteem.

Understanding Self-Esteem

Self-esteem refers to the overall subjective evaluation of one's worth, capabilities, and value as an individual. It encompasses beliefs about oneself and plays a fundamental role in shaping our thoughts, emotions, and behaviors. Developing healthy self-esteem is crucial for individuals to withstand the negative effects of bullying and to cultivate resilience in the face of adversity.

Effects of Bullying on Self-Esteem

Bullying can have a significant impact on an individual's self-esteem, leading to feelings of worthlessness, shame, and self-doubt. Constant negative interactions and derogatory comments can erode self-confidence and create a distorted self-perception. It is essential to address these effects and provide support to individuals who have experienced bullying, helping them rebuild and strengthen their self-esteem.

Techniques for Building Self-Esteem:

a. Self-Acceptance: Encouraging individuals to accept and embrace their unique qualities and strengths is a vital step in building self-esteem. Emphasizing self-acceptance allows individuals to recognize their inherent worthiness and value as individuals.

b. Positive Self-Talk: Guiding individuals to replace negative self-talk with positive and affirming statements can significantly impact their self-esteem. Encouraging individuals to challenge negative thoughts, reframe them positively, and focus on their strengths and accomplishments promotes a healthier self-image.

c. Setting Achievable Goals: Setting realistic and attainable goals helps individuals develop a sense of competence and accomplishment. By breaking down larger goals into smaller, manageable steps, individuals can build confidence as they make progress and achieve milestones.

d. Encouraging Healthy Relationships: Nurturing positive relationships with supportive friends, family members, and mentors can foster a sense of belonging and validation. Surrounding oneself with individuals who uplift and encourage them can contribute to a positive self-image.

e. Recognizing Achievements: Celebrating personal achievements, no matter how small, reinforces a positive self-perception. Encouraging individuals to acknowledge and celebrate their accomplishments enhances self-esteem and self-belief.

f. Developing Coping Strategies: Teaching individuals effective coping strategies, such as problem-solving, resilience-building techniques, and stress management, equips them with the tools to navigate challenging situations and maintain a positive self-image.

g. Seeking Professional Help: In cases where low self-esteem persists despite efforts to improve, seeking professional support from counselors or therapists trained in self-esteem building can provide valuable guidance and assistance.

Building self-esteem is a crucial component in addressing and combating bullying. By nurturing a strong sense of self-worth, individuals are better equipped to withstand the negative impact of bullying, develop resilience, and foster a positive self-image. Through techniques such as self-acceptance, positive self-talk, goal setting, and cultivating healthy relationships, individuals can build and enhance their self-esteem. By promoting self-esteem, we empower individuals to stand up against bullying, embrace their unique qualities, and thrive in the face of adversity. Together, let us create a culture that values and supports the self-esteem of all individuals, fostering a safer and more inclusive environment for everyone.

SECTION B: CONFLICT RESOLUTION

Conflict is a natural part of human interaction, and addressing conflicts effectively is crucial in the context of bullying prevention. Conflict resolution skills empower individuals to navigate challenging situations, assert their needs, and seek peaceful resolutions. In this section, we will explore the importance of conflict resolution in addressing bullying, techniques for effective conflict resolution, and strategies for promoting positive interpersonal relationships.

Understanding Conflict Resolution

Conflict resolution refers to the process of addressing conflicts in a constructive and peaceful manner. It involves listening to different perspectives, finding common ground, and seeking mutually beneficial solutions. By equipping individuals with conflict resolution skills, we empower them to navigate conflicts assertively, fostering healthier relationships and preventing escalation.

Conflict Resolution in Bullying Situations

In the context of bullying, conflict resolution plays a critical role in addressing and preventing further harm. It allows individuals to assert their boundaries, communicate their concerns, and work towards a resolution. Effective conflict resolution can reduce aggression, restore trust, and promote a safe and respectful environment.

Techniques for Conflict Resolution:

a. Active Listening: Active listening involves fully engaging with the other person's perspective, demonstrating empathy, and seeking to understand their feelings and needs. By actively listening, individuals can foster open communication and create a safe space for resolving conflicts.

b. Assertive Communication: Assertive communication is key in conflict resolution. It involves expressing one's needs, concerns, and boundaries in a clear and respectful manner. Teaching individuals assertive communication skills empowers them to address conflicts directly and assert their rights.

c. Collaborative Problem-Solving: Collaborative problem-solving focuses on finding mutually beneficial solutions to conflicts. It involves identifying shared goals, brainstorming creative alternatives, and working together toward a resolution that meets the needs of all parties involved.

d. Emotional Regulation: Emotional regulation is crucial in conflict resolution, as heightened emotions can escalate conflicts. Teaching individuals strategies for managing and expressing emotions constructively, such as deep breathing, mindfulness techniques, and self-reflection, helps maintain a calm and rational approach during conflicts.

e. Mediation and Negotiation: Mediation involves the intervention of a neutral third party to facilitate communication and negotiation between conflicting parties. Mediators help individuals find common ground, explore different perspectives, and work toward a mutually agreeable resolution.

f. Conflict Resolution Strategies: Providing individuals with a range of conflict resolution strategies, such as compromise, problem-solving, and seeking advice from trusted adults, equips them with a toolbox of approaches to address conflicts effectively.

Restorative Justice Practices: Restorative justice practices focus on repairing harm, promoting empathy, and fostering understanding between conflicting parties. These practices encourage dialogue, accountability, and healing, creating an opportunity for growth and reconciliation.

Conflict resolution skills are essential in addressing and preventing bullying situations. By teaching individuals techniques such as active listening, assertive communication, collaborative problem-solving, and emotional regulation, we empower them to navigate conflicts peacefully and assert their rights. Mediation, negotiation, and restorative justice practices provide additional tools for resolving conflicts in a fair and inclusive manner. By promoting conflict resolution, we foster healthier relationships, prevent further harm, and create a positive and inclusive environment. Together, let us equip individuals with the skills to resolve conflicts effectively, promoting empathy, understanding, and peaceful resolutions in the face of bullying and adversity.

SECTION C: SOCIAL SKILLS TRAINING

In the face of bullying, social skills training plays a vital role in empowering individuals to navigate social interactions confidently and effectively. By equipping individuals with essential social skills, we can foster healthy relationships, build resilience, and create a supportive environment. In this section, we will explore the importance of social skills training in addressing bullying, key social skills to develop, and strategies to enhance social competence.

The Importance of Social Skills Training

Social skills are fundamental for positive social interactions and healthy relationships. Social skills training provides individuals with the knowledge, strategies, and practice needed to navigate various social situations, assert boundaries, and communicate effectively. By developing these skills, individuals can cultivate self-confidence, empathy, and the ability to establish and maintain healthy relationships.

Key Social Skills to Develop:

a. Effective Communication: Effective communication is essential for expressing thoughts, feelings, and needs clearly and assertively. It involves active listening, using appropriate body language, and choosing words wisely to ensure understanding and mutual respect.

b. Empathy and Perspective-Taking: Empathy allows individuals to understand and share the feelings of others. By practicing empathy, individuals can build meaningful connections, develop compassion, and respond with kindness and understanding.

c. Assertiveness: Being assertive involves expressing oneself honestly, directly, and respectfully, while considering the rights and feelings of others. Developing assertiveness skills empowers individuals to establish boundaries, stand up against bullying, and advocate for themselves and others.

d. Problem-Solving: Problem-solving skills enable individuals to approach conflicts and challenges constructively. By learning effective problem-solving techniques, individuals can identify solutions, evaluate consequences, and make informed decisions to resolve issues peacefully.

e. Conflict Resolution: Conflict resolution skills allow individuals to address conflicts in a peaceful and respectful manner. By learning strategies such as active listening, negotiation, and compromise, individuals can navigate conflicts, promote understanding, and build mutually beneficial resolutions.

f. Emotional Regulation: Emotional regulation skills help individuals manage their emotions in social situations. By understanding and controlling their emotions, individuals can respond appropriately, maintain composure, and prevent conflicts from escalating.

g. Empowering Peer Interactions: Developing social skills also involves fostering positive peer interactions. Encouraging inclusivity, empathy, and respect among peers creates a supportive environment where everyone feels valued and accepted.

Strategies for Enhancing Social Competence:

a. Social Skills Training Programs: Utilizing evidence-based social skills training programs designed for specific age groups can provide structured guidance and practice in developing essential social skills.

b. Role-Playing and Modeling: Engaging in role-playing activities and observing positive social interactions through modeling can help individuals learn and practice effective social skills in a safe and controlled environment.

c. Group Activities and Team Building: Participating in group activities and team-building exercises promotes collaboration, communication, and cooperation, fostering social skills and a sense of belonging.

d. Peer Support and Mentoring: Creating opportunities for peer support and mentoring encourages positive social interactions and provides guidance for individuals to learn from their peers' experiences and perspectives.

e. Community Engagement: Involving individuals in community service and engagement activities promote social responsibility, empathy, and the development of social skills through meaningful interactions with diverse populations.

f. Continuous Practice and Feedback: Regularly practicing social skills and seeking feedback from trusted adults, mentors, or peers can help individuals refine their abilities and build confidence in their social interactions.

Social skills training is a valuable tool in addressing bullying and building resilience among individuals. By focusing on effective communication, empathy, assertiveness, problem-solving, conflict resolution, emotional regulation, and empowering peer interactions, we equip individuals with the skills needed to navigate social situations confidently and establish healthy relationships.

Chapter 5: <u>Social Media</u> Navigating the Digital Landscape for Healthy Engagement and Well-being

In today's interconnected world, social media has become an integral part of our lives, especially for teenagers. However, it is essential to approach social media with intention and mindfulness to ensure a positive and balanced experience. This chapter explores three key areas: setting boundaries, mindful social media use, and digital footprint management. By understanding and implementing these strategies, you can harness the power of social media while safeguarding your emotional well-being and building a positive online presence. Let's dive into these important topics and discover how to navigate the digital world with confidence and resilience.

SECTION A: SETTING BOUNDARIES

In today's digital age, social media has become an integral part of our daily lives, especially for teenagers. While it offers numerous opportunities for connection and self-expression, it also presents challenges that can impact our emotional well-being. One crucial aspect of maintaining a healthy relationship with social media is setting boundaries. By establishing clear limits and guidelines for our online engagement, we can cultivate a positive and balanced experience that promotes emotional wellness and resilience. In this section, we will explore the importance of setting boundaries in the digital world and provide practical techniques and strategies to help teenagers navigate social media with confidence and intention.

Understanding the Need for Boundaries

Social media platforms provide a constant stream of information and interactions, making it easy to become overwhelmed and lose track of time. Without proper boundaries, excessive use of social media can lead to anxiety, stress, and a sense of being disconnected from the real world. Setting boundaries helps individuals regain control over their online activities and create a healthier balance between the virtual and physical realms.

Establishing Personal Boundaries

The first step in setting boundaries is understanding our individual needs and limitations. This involves recognizing how social media affects our emotional well-being, identifying triggers or negative patterns, and determining the desired level of engagement. By reflecting on our values, priorities, and personal goals, we can establish boundaries that align with our overall well-being and promote a healthy relationship with social media.

Limiting Screen Time

One effective way to set boundaries is by regulating the amount of time spent on social media. Establishing specific time limits and creating a schedule for digital usage helps ensure a balanced and productive approach to online engagement. By designating certain periods for social media activities and dedicating time for offline pursuits, such as hobbies, exercise, or face-to-face interactions, individuals can maintain a sense of control and prevent excessive reliance on virtual connections.

Defining Social Media Usage Guidelines

In addition to managing screen time, it is crucial to establish guidelines for social media usage. This includes determining the types of content we consume, the accounts we follow, and the platforms we engage with. By consciously curating our digital environment, we can ensure that our social media feeds are filled with positive and meaningful content that aligns with our values and interests. It also involves being selective about accepting friend requests or connections and setting privacy settings that protect our personal information.

Creating Digital-Free Zones and Times

To further enforce boundaries, it can be beneficial to establish digital-free zones and times. This means designating specific areas or moments in our lives where electronic devices are not allowed, such as during meals, family gatherings, or before bedtime. By carving out spaces and moments dedicated to unplugging from the digital world, we create opportunities for genuine connections, self-reflection, and relaxation, fostering a healthier balance between online and offline experiences.

Handling FOMO (Fear of Missing Out)

One common challenge when setting boundaries is managing the fear of missing out (FOMO). Social media often showcases highlights and curated moments of others' lives, leading to feelings of inadequacy or exclusion. It is essential to recognize that social media presents a filtered version of reality and that everyone experiences ups and downs. By practicing self-compassion, focusing on our own growth and achievements, and cultivating gratitude for the present moment, we can overcome FOMO and embrace the joy and richness of our own lives.

Setting boundaries is a fundamental aspect of managing social media usage and promoting emotional wellness in the digital age. By establishing personal boundaries, limiting screen time, defining usage guidelines, creating digital-free zones, and addressing FOMO, teenagers can navigate the online world with intention and balance. These practices empower individuals to make conscious choices about their social media engagement, protect their emotional well-being, and cultivate resilience in the face of the digital landscape's challenges. By prioritizing self-care and mindful engagement, teenagers can harness the benefits of social media while mitigating its potential negative impacts.

In conclusion, setting boundaries is a vital skill for teenagers to develop as they navigate the digital world. By understanding the need for boundaries, establishing personal limits, and implementing practical strategies, young individuals can foster a healthy relationships with social media. Setting boundaries allows for intentional and balanced engagement, ensuring emotional wellness, promoting healthy habits, and building resilience. By taking control of their digital lives, teenagers can embrace the positive aspects of social media while safeguarding their well-being in the digital age. "Unplugged: A Practical Guide to Managing Teenage Stress in the Digital Age" equips teenagers with the knowledge and tools they need to set effective boundaries and thrive in the ever-evolving digital landscape.

SECTION B: MINDFUL SOCIAL MEDIA USE

In today's digital age, social media has become an integral part of teenagers' lives. It offers opportunities for connection, self-expression, and access to information. However, the excessive use and misuse of social media can also have detrimental effects on teenagers' mental health, self-esteem, and overall well-being. To navigate the digital landscape successfully, it is crucial for teenagers to develop mindful social media use habits. This section of "Unplugged: A Practical Guide to Managing Teenage Stress in the Digital Age" explores the importance of mindfulness and provides strategies for using social media in a conscious and balanced way.

Understanding Mindful Social Media Use

Mindful social media use involves being present, intentional, and aware of the impact that digital interactions can have on mental and emotional well-being. It requires teenagers to cultivate self-awareness, set boundaries, and make informed choices about their online activities. By practicing mindfulness while engaging with social media, teenagers can reduce stress, enhance their digital well-being, and foster healthy relationships with technology.

Strategies for Mindful Social Media Use:

a. Self-Assessment and Reflection:

Encouraging teenagers to reflect on their motivations, emotions, and behaviors related to social media can help them gain insight into their digital habits. They can ask themselves questions like: How does social media make me feel? How much time am I spending on social media? What are my intentions when using social media? This self-awareness lays the foundation for mindful engagement.

b. Setting Intentional Goals:

Helping teenagers set clear and meaningful goals for their social media use can guide them toward more purposeful interactions. Examples of goals could include connecting with friends and family, pursuing hobbies or interests, or seeking inspiration and learning. By aligning their actions with their intentions, teenagers can avoid mindless scrolling and focus on activities that bring value and fulfillment.

c. Practicing Digital Detox:

Encouraging regular breaks from social media is crucial for maintaining a healthy balance. Designating specific periods of time or activities when social media is off-limits can provide space for self-reflection, creativity, and face-to-face interactions. Teenagers can explore alternative activities such as reading, exercising, engaging in hobbies, or spending quality time with loved ones.

d. Cultivating Mindfulness Techniques:

Introducing teenagers to mindfulness practices can help them develop a deeper sense of presence and awareness while using social media. Techniques like deep breathing, grounding exercises, and mindfulness meditation can help teenagers stay centered, manage stress, and avoid getting caught up in comparison or negative emotions triggered by social media.

e. Curating a Positive Online Environment:
Encouraging teenagers to curate their social media feeds and connections can significantly impact their well-being. They can unfollow accounts that promote unrealistic standards, negativity, or toxicity. Instead, they can seek out accounts that inspire, educate, and uplift. Engaging with positive and meaningful content can contribute to a more positive digital experience.

f. Practicing Digital Citizenship:

Teaching teenagers about responsible digital citizenship is crucial for promoting respectful and ethical behavior online. They should be aware of the consequences of their actions, such as cyberbullying, spreading misinformation, or engaging in harmful online trends. By practicing empathy, kindness, and critical thinking, teenagers can contribute to a healthier and more supportive online community.

g. Balancing Online and Offline Life:

Emphasizing the importance of maintaining a balance between online and offline activities is essential for teenagers' well-being. Encouraging them to engage in hobbies, spend time outdoors, nurture real-world relationships, and pursue offline interests can provide a sense of fulfillment and reduce the reliance on social media as the primary source of validation and connection.

Mindful social media use is a transformative practice that empowers teenagers to navigate the digital landscape with intention, awareness, and balance. By incorporating the strategies outlined in this section of "Unplugged: A Practical Guide to Managing Teenage Stress in the Digital Age," teenagers can develop healthier and more meaningful relationships with social media. They will learn to prioritize their mental and emotional well-being, set boundaries, and make conscious choices about their digital interactions. Mindful social media use promotes self-awareness, fosters positive online environments, and encourages responsible digital citizenship. By practicing mindfulness, teenagers can avoid the pitfalls of excessive screen time, comparison, and cyberbullying. Instead, they can harness the potential of social media to connect, inspire, and learn. With the tools and knowledge gained from this section, teenagers will be equipped to use social media as a tool for growth, self-expression, and meaningful connection, while maintaining a healthy balance between their online and offline lives. The journey towards mindful social media use starts with self-reflection, intentionality, and a commitment to digital well-being. By embracing these practices, teenagers can thrive in the digital age and create a positive and fulfilling relationship with social media.

SECTION C: DIGITAL FOOTPRINT MANAGEMENT

In this digital age, where our online presence plays a significant role in our lives, managing our digital footprint has become essential for maintaining healthy engagement and overall well-being. Your digital footprint consists of the information you leave behind as you navigate the online world, including your social media activities, online interactions, and the content you share. Being mindful of your digital footprint can help you protect your privacy, build a positive online reputation, and foster a healthy relationship with technology.

Here are some proven techniques to effectively manage your digital footprint:

a. Reflect on Your Digital Identity: Start by reflecting on the kind of digital identity you want to cultivate. Consider the values, interests, and beliefs you want to project online. Ask yourself if your digital presence aligns with your authentic self. Remember that you have control over the image you present, and it's important to be genuine and consistent with your values across different online platforms.

b. Set Privacy Preferences: Most social media platforms offer privacy settings that allow you to control who can see your posts and personal information. Take the time to review and customize these settings according to your comfort level. Restrict access to your profile to only trusted friends and family and be cautious about accepting friend requests from strangers. Regularly revisit your privacy settings as platforms may update their policies over time.

c. Think Before You Share: Before posting anything online, consider the potential consequences and implications. Once something is shared, it can be challenging to completely remove it from the digital world. Ask yourself if the content is appropriate, respectful, and aligns with your values. Remember, sharing personal information such as your address, phone number, or financial details can compromise your privacy and safety.

d. Maintain Digital Etiquette: Practice good digital etiquette by treating others with respect and kindness in your online interactions. Avoid engaging in cyberbullying, spreading rumors, or participating in negative conversations. Remember that your words have an impact on others, and fostering a positive online environment contributes to a healthier digital landscape.

e. Regularly Review Your Social Media Presence: Take the time to review your social media profiles and posts periodically. Remove any content that no longer aligns with your current values or could be misinterpreted. Ensure that your profile reflects the best version of yourself and promotes positivity. It's also a good practice to Google your name occasionally to see what information is associated with you online.

f. Seek Support from Trusted Adults: If you encounter any online harassment, inappropriate behavior, or concerns regarding your digital footprint, don't hesitate to reach out to a trusted adult for guidance and support. They can provide valuable advice and help you navigate challenging situations effectively.

By managing your digital footprint thoughtfully, you can harness the benefits of social media while protecting your privacy and emotional well-being. Remember, the online world is a powerful tool, and using it responsibly contributes to a healthier and more fulfilling digital experience.

NOTES

Chapter 6: <u>Political Climate</u>
Finding Common Ground: Building Bridges in a Divided Political Climate

SECTION A: PROVIDING DIVERSE PERSPECTIVES

In the modern world, where political opinions and ideologies can often polarize communities, it is crucial for young people to develop the ability to understand and appreciate diverse perspectives. The section on "Providing Diverse Perspectives" in the book "Unplugged: A Practical Guide to Managing Teenage Stress in the Digital Age" equips teenagers with the tools they need to navigate the complexities of the political landscape. This section emphasizes the importance of seeking out and considering a wide range of viewpoints, fostering empathy, and cultivating a nuanced understanding of the world. By providing practical techniques and thought-provoking exercises, the book empowers readers to engage in respectful and meaningful conversations, challenge their own assumptions, and develop a more comprehensive understanding of complex issues.

Embracing Diversity

In this chapter, readers are introduced to the concept of embracing diversity in political discourse. They learn that individuals' backgrounds, experiences, and beliefs shape their perspectives and that genuine understanding can only be achieved by engaging with a wide range of voices. Through case studies and real-life examples, readers are introduced to individuals who have overcome biases and prejudices, promoting inclusivity and fostering a sense of unity within diverse communities.

Empathy and Perspective-Taking

Building empathy and practicing perspective-taking are essential skills for navigating the political landscape. This section provides practical exercises and techniques to help readers develop these skills. By encouraging readers to step into the shoes of others and understand their motivations, fears, and aspirations, the book promotes empathy as a tool for fostering open-mindedness and promoting productive conversations. Through guided reflection and interactive activities, readers gain a deeper appreciation for the importance of empathy in bridging political divides.

Active Listening and Constructive Dialogue

Effective communication is key to understanding diverse perspectives. This section emphasizes the value of active listening and constructive dialogue in the context of political discussions. Readers learn strategies for active listening, such as paraphrasing, asking open-ended questions, and validating others' experiences. The book also provides guidelines for engaging in respectful and constructive dialogue, emphasizing the importance of patience, mutual respect, and the willingness to learn from others. By honing these communication skills, readers can contribute to meaningful conversations that promote understanding and bridge political gaps.

Media Literacy and Critical Thinking

A critical aspect of providing diverse perspectives involves navigating the media landscape with a discerning eye. This section delves into the importance of media literacy and critical thinking when consuming and interpreting political information. Readers are introduced to strategies for evaluating sources, detecting bias, and fact-checking information. By equipping young readers with the tools to critically analyze media content, the book empowers them to form well-informed opinions and engage in informed discussions based on reliable information.

Encouraging Civil Discourse

Civil discourse is essential for fostering an environment where diverse perspectives can be heard and respected. This section of the book focuses on promoting civil discourse by highlighting the importance of respectful language, avoiding personal attacks, and focusing on issues rather than individuals. Through case studies and examples of successful civil discourse, readers gain insights into how constructive conversations can lead to meaningful progress and positive change. By learning to navigate disagreements respectfully and constructively, readers develop skills that can contribute to building bridges in a divided political climate.

Exploring Cultural Differences

Understanding and appreciating cultural differences is crucial for providing diverse perspectives. This section explores how cultural backgrounds can shape political beliefs and attitudes. Readers are encouraged to explore different cultural perspectives, challenging their own biases and broadening their understanding of global issues. Through engaging narratives and cross-cultural comparisons, readers gain a deeper appreciation for the complexity of political dynamics and the importance of cultural competence in fostering diverse perspectives.

Navigating Political Controversies

Political controversies can often be emotionally charged and divisive. This section equips readers with strategies for navigating such contentious topics while maintaining open-mindedness and respect for differing opinions. Readers learn techniques for staying calm and composed during heated discussions, reframing conversations to focus on common goals, and finding areas of compromise. By exploring case studies and engaging in role-playing exercises, readers develop the skills needed to navigate political controversies in a constructive and empathetic manner.

Promoting Civic Engagement

Promoting civic engagement is a key aspect of providing diverse perspectives. This section highlights the importance of active participation in the political process, from voting in elections to engaging in grassroots movements. Readers learn about the power of collective action, the impact of community involvement, and the significance of being informed and engaged citizens. By empowering readers to participate in shaping their communities and advocating for the causes they believe in, the book encourages the promotion of diverse perspectives in the political sphere.

Building Bridges Across Divides

In a politically divided climate, building bridges becomes crucial for fostering understanding and collaboration. This section focuses on practical strategies for building bridges across political divides. Readers explore methods for finding common ground, identifying shared values, and seeking compromise. Through real-life examples and interactive exercises, readers develop the skills needed to bridge ideological gaps and work towards constructive solutions. By emphasizing the power of collaboration and finding common goals, the book empowers readers to contribute to positive change in their communities.

"Finding Common Ground: Building Bridges in a Divided Political Climate" offers a comprehensive approach to navigating the complexities of the political landscape. By providing diverse perspectives, promoting media literacy, and fostering open-mindedness, readers gain the tools necessary to engage in meaningful and respectful political discourse. This chapter encourages readers to embrace empathy, actively listen to others, and critically analyze information. By doing so, readers can contribute to a more inclusive and

understanding society where diverse perspectives are valued
and respected. With the guidance and techniques provided in
this chapter, readers are empowered to become informed and
engaged citizens who can bridge political divides and work
towards positive change in the world.

SECTION B: PROMOTE MEDIA LITERACY

In today's digital age, where information is readily accessible
and quickly shared, media literacy is essential for teenagers to
navigate the political climate. This section of the book,
"Finding Common Ground: Building Bridges in a Divided
Political Climate," emphasizes the importance of media
literacy and equips readers with the necessary skills to
critically analyze and evaluate media sources.

Understanding Media Bias

Media bias is a pervasive issue that can significantly impact
individuals' perceptions and understanding of political events.
This section delves into the concept of media bias and
explores strategies for identifying and interpreting biased
information. Readers learn to recognize different forms of
bias, such as political, ideological, and sensational bias, and
understand how it can shape public opinion. By developing a
keen awareness of media bias, readers are empowered to

seek out diverse sources of information and form well-rounded perspectives.

Evaluating News Sources

In an era of misinformation and fake news, it is crucial for teenagers to discern reliable and trustworthy news sources. This section provides readers with tools and techniques to evaluate the credibility and accuracy of news outlets. Topics covered include fact-checking methods, cross-referencing information, and analyzing the reputation and track record of news organizations. By teaching readers how to critically evaluate news sources, the book promotes media literacy and helps readers make informed decisions about the information they consume and share.

Recognizing Manipulative Techniques

In today's media landscape, manipulative techniques are employed to shape public opinion and advance specific agendas. This section explores common manipulative techniques, such as emotional appeals, loaded language, and selective framing. Readers learn to recognize these techniques and become more resistant to their influence. By understanding how manipulation works, readers can develop a discerning eye and become active consumers of media, effectively separating fact from fiction.

Engaging in Responsible Social Media Use

Social media platforms play a significant role in shaping political discourse and public opinion. This section addresses the impact of social media on political engagement and provides strategies for responsible social media use. Readers learn about the echo chamber effect, filter bubbles, and the dangers of misinformation on social media. They also gain insights into fostering respectful online discussions, fact-checking information before sharing, and avoiding the spread of harmful rumors. By promoting responsible social media use, the book empowers readers to engage in meaningful and informed conversations that bridge political divides.

Developing Critical Thinking Skills

At the core of media literacy is the development of critical thinking skills. This section focuses on enhancing readers' critical thinking abilities, enabling them to approach media content with a discerning and analytical mindset. Readers learn to question assumptions, identify logical fallacies, and evaluate arguments. By honing these critical thinking skills, readers can independently analyze political information, weigh different perspectives, and form well-reasoned opinions.

Promoting media literacy is crucial in today's politically charged and digitally connected world. "Finding Common Ground: Building Bridges in a Divided Political Climate" empowers readers to become critical consumers of media, adept at identifying bias, evaluating news sources, and recognizing manipulative techniques. By promoting responsible social media use and developing critical thinking skills, readers are equipped to engage with political content in a thoughtful and informed manner. With media literacy as a foundation, teenagers can actively participate in political discussions, challenge misinformation, and contribute to a more inclusive and well-informed society.

SECTION C: FOSTER OPEN-MINDNESS

In a polarized political climate, fostering open-mindedness is crucial for teenagers to navigate diverse perspectives and engage in constructive conversations. This section of the book, "Finding Common Ground: Building Bridges in a Divided Political Climate," emphasizes the importance of open-mindedness and provides practical strategies for cultivating this mindset.

Embracing Diversity of Thought

Open-mindedness begins with embracing the diversity of

thought. This section encourages readers to value different perspectives and recognize the richness that diversity brings to political discussions. It explores the concept of cognitive diversity, highlighting how diverse perspectives can lead to innovative solutions and deeper understanding. By appreciating and seeking out diverse viewpoints, readers can broaden their own horizons and develop a more nuanced understanding of complex political issues.

Practicing Empathy

Empathy plays a vital role in fostering open-mindedness. This section delves into the importance of empathy in political conversations and provides strategies for cultivating empathy towards those with different beliefs. Readers learn techniques for active listening, putting themselves in others' shoes, and seeking common ground. By practicing empathy, readers can approach political discussions with compassion and understanding, creating a more conducive environment for dialogue and collaboration.

Developing Reflective Thinking

Reflective thinking is a critical skill for fostering open-mindedness. This section encourages readers to engage in introspection and self-reflection, questioning their own biases and assumptions. Readers learn techniques for examining their own beliefs and considering alternative viewpoints. By engaging in reflective thinking, readers can challenge their own biases, expand their perspectives, and develop a more balanced approach to political discussions.

Encouraging Civil Discourse

Civil discourse is essential for fostering open-mindedness and constructive political engagement. This section provides readers with guidelines for engaging in respectful and productive conversations. It explores strategies for active listening, expressing ideas respectfully, and managing conflict in a constructive manner. By promoting civil discourse, readers can create a space where diverse perspectives are welcomed and respected, leading to more meaningful and fruitful discussions.

Seeking Common Ground

In a divided political climate, seeking common ground is a powerful way to foster open-mindedness. This section explores techniques for finding shared values and interests amidst differing opinions. Readers learn strategies for finding common goals and working towards collaborative solutions. By seeking common ground, readers can bridge divides, build relationships, and promote a more inclusive and united political landscape.

Fostering open-mindedness is vital for teenagers to navigate the complexities of a divided political climate. "Finding Common Ground: Building Bridges in a Divided Political Climate" equips readers with the tools and strategies to embrace the diversity of thought, practice empathy, engage in reflective thinking, encourage civil discourse, and seek common ground. By cultivating open-mindedness, readers can approach political discussions with humility, respect, and a genuine desire to understand diverse perspectives. In doing so, they contribute to a more inclusive, tolerant, and cooperative society, where dialogue and collaboration can thrive.

NOTES

Chapter 7: <u>Trauma</u> Understanding the Impact of Trauma: Building a Foundation for Recovery

Welcome to Chapter 7 of "Unplugged: A Practical Guide to Managing Teenage Stress in the Digital Age." In this chapter, titled "Understanding the Impact of Trauma: Building a Foundation for Recovery," we delve into the profound effects of trauma on teenagers and provide valuable insights and techniques to help them navigate the path to healing and resilience. Within this chapter, we will explore three key sections that are integral to the recovery process: Professional Counseling, Creative Expression, and Physical Exercise. By understanding the impact of trauma, seeking professional help, exploring creative outlets, and engaging in physical activities, teenagers can begin to rebuild their emotional well-being and lay the foundation for a brighter future. Join us as we embark on this transformative journey of healing and growth.

SECTION A: PROFESSIONAL COUNSELING

When teenagers experience trauma, it can have a profound impact on their emotional well-being and overall quality of life.

Professional counseling plays a crucial role in helping teenagers navigate the complexities of trauma, providing them with the necessary support and guidance to heal and build resilience. In this section, we will explore the benefits and importance of professional counseling for teenagers facing trauma in the digital age. We will delve into the various therapeutic approaches and techniques used by counselors to address trauma-related issues and promote emotional well-being. By seeking professional counseling, teenagers can embark on a transformative journey toward recovery and develop the skills needed to thrive in the face of adversity.

The Role of Professional Counselors

Professional counselors are trained experts who specialize in helping individuals cope with trauma and its aftermath. They provide a safe and supportive environment for teenagers to express their feelings, thoughts, and experiences. Counselors offer a non-judgmental space where teenagers can explore their emotions and develop healthy coping mechanisms. Through their expertise, counselors guide teenagers in understanding and processing their trauma, helping them regain a sense of control and empowerment over their lives.

Tailored Approaches for Trauma

Professional counselors utilize various therapeutic

approaches tailored to meet the unique needs of teenagers who have experienced trauma. These approaches may include cognitive-behavioral therapy (CBT), trauma-focused therapy, eye movement desensitization and reprocessing (EMDR), and mindfulness-based techniques. These evidence-based practices aim to address the specific symptoms and challenges associated with trauma, such as anxiety, depression, intrusive thoughts, and difficulty with emotional regulation. Counselors work collaboratively with teenagers to develop personalized treatment plans that focus on their strengths, goals, and individual circumstances.

Building Resilience and Coping Skills

One of the primary objectives of professional counseling is to help teenagers build resilience and develop effective coping skills. Through therapy sessions, counselors assist teenagers in identifying and understanding their triggers, managing stress, and developing healthy ways to cope with emotional distress. Counselors provide guidance on relaxation techniques, problem-solving strategies, and self-care practices that empower teenagers to navigate challenges and setbacks with resilience and confidence. By acquiring these skills, teenagers can not only overcome the immediate effects of trauma but also develop lifelong tools for managing stress and promoting their emotional well-being.

Establishing Support Systems

Professional counseling also helps teenagers establish and strengthen their support systems. Counselors may facilitate family therapy sessions to improve communication and understanding within the family unit. Additionally, they can assist teenagers in connecting with peer support groups or other community resources where they can share experiences, gain validation, and receive support from individuals who have gone through similar challenges. By fostering healthy relationships and building a network of support, teenagers can feel less isolated and more empowered to cope with trauma and its aftermath. Professional counseling plays a vital role in helping teenagers recover from trauma and develop the resilience needed to thrive in the digital age. Through the guidance of trained professionals, teenagers can navigate the complexities of their experiences, process their emotions, and acquire the necessary coping skills. By seeking professional counseling, teenagers can find solace, support, and a renewed sense of hope on their journey toward healing and resilience. Remember, reaching out for help is not a sign of weakness but a courageous step toward a brighter future.

SECTION B: CREATIVE EXPRESSION

In the aftermath of trauma, finding healthy outlets for emotional expression is crucial for teenagers' healing and recovery. The creative expression serves as a powerful tool for teenagers to process their emotions, explore their inner world, and communicate their experiences in a safe and empowering way. In this section, we will delve into the transformative potential of creative expression as a therapeutic modality for teenagers facing trauma in the digital age. We will explore various forms of creative expressions, such as art, music, writing, and drama, and examine how they can facilitate healing, promote self-discovery, and foster resilience.

Art as Therapy

Art therapy offers teenagers a means of expressing and exploring their emotions and experiences visually. Through painting, drawing, sculpting, or other artistic mediums, teenagers can tap into their subconscious, allowing their emotions to surface and find tangible form. Art therapy provides a non-verbal and symbolic language that can bypass the limitations of traditional verbal expression, enabling teenagers to communicate their innermost feelings and experiences. Engaging in art therapy not only provides a sense of catharsis but also allows for self-reflection, self-discovery, and a deeper understanding of their trauma and its impact.

Music as Healing

Music has the power to evoke emotions, create connections, and serve as a therapeutic outlet for teenagers facing trauma. Whether through playing an instrument, singing, or listening to music, teenagers can find solace, solace, and empowerment. Music therapy enables teenagers to express themselves, process complex emotions, and find comfort in the rhythms and melodies. It can serve as a form of self-expression, emotional release, and a source of inspiration and hope. Music therapy also offers opportunities for connection and collaboration, fostering a sense of belonging and support.

Writing for Reflection

Writing can be a transformative medium for teenagers to reflect on their experiences, make sense of their emotions, and gain clarity. Journaling, poetry, storytelling, or even writing letters to themselves or others can provide a space for teenagers to process their thoughts, document their journey, and explore their inner world. Writing allows for self-reflection, introspection, and the development of a narrative that can help teenagers gain perspective, find meaning, and foster self-compassion. Through written expression, teenagers can externalize their trauma, release emotions, and create a sense of empowerment and agency.

Drama and Role-Playing

Drama and role-playing provide teenagers with an opportunity to step into different roles and perspectives, allowing them to explore their trauma from alternative angles. Through acting, improvisation, or role-playing exercises, teenagers can safely reenact and examine their experiences, gaining insight and understanding. Drama therapy encourages teenagers to embody and express their emotions, confront their fears, and practice new ways of responding to challenging situations. It offers a platform for building confidence, developing empathy, and promoting resilience.

The creative expression serves as a powerful and transformative tool for teenagers to heal, process trauma, and build resilience in the digital age. Whether through art, music, writing, or drama, creative outlets provide teenagers with a safe and empowering space to explore their emotions, communicate their experiences, and find healing. Engaging in creative expression allows teenagers to tap into their inner strength, discover new perspectives, and develop healthy coping mechanisms. By embracing their creativity, teenagers can embark on a journey of self-discovery, growth, and healing, reclaiming their voice and empowering themselves to thrive beyond trauma.

SECTION C: PHYSICAL EXERCISE

Physical exercise plays a vital role in the healing and recovery process for teenagers who have experienced trauma. Engaging in regular physical activity not only benefits physical well-being but also has a profound impact on mental and emotional well-being. In this section, we will explore the significance of physical exercise as a therapeutic tool for teenagers facing trauma in the digital age. We will delve into the various ways in which exercise can promote resilience, reduce stress, enhance self-esteem, and contribute to overall emotional wellness.

The Mind-Body Connection

Physical exercise establishes a powerful mind-body connection that can positively influence teenagers' emotional well-being. When engaging in exercise, the brain releases endorphins, also known as "feel-good" chemicals, which help alleviate stress, reduce anxiety, and boost mood. Regular exercise can help regulate emotions, improve sleep patterns, and increase energy levels, all of which are crucial for teenagers recovering from trauma. By engaging in physical activity, teenagers can cultivate a sense of empowerment, control, and resilience.

Stress Reduction and Emotional Regulation

Trauma often leads to heightened stress levels and difficulties in managing emotions. Physical exercise provides a healthy outlet for stress release and emotional regulation. Whether through cardiovascular exercises, strength training, yoga, or other forms of physical activity, teenagers can channel their pent-up emotions into constructive energy. Exercise serves as a natural stress reliever, promoting a sense of calm, reducing anxiety, and enhancing emotional stability. By incorporating regular physical exercise into their routine, teenagers can develop effective coping mechanisms and build resilience in the face of trauma.

Self-Esteem and Body Image

Trauma can significantly impact teenagers' self-esteem and body image. Engaging in physical exercise can help foster a positive body image and improve self-esteem. Regular physical activity helps teenagers develop a sense of strength, competence, and accomplishment. As they set and achieve fitness goals, they gain confidence in their physical abilities, leading to a more positive perception of their bodies and overall self-worth. Physical exercise also offers an opportunity for teenagers to engage in healthy competition, teamwork, and social interaction, further boosting their self-esteem and sense of belonging.

Empowerment and Resilience

Physical exercise promotes a sense of empowerment and resilience among teenagers facing trauma. By pushing their physical limits and achieving new milestones, teenagers build a sense of resilience and belief in their ability to overcome challenges. Engaging in regular exercise empowers teenagers to take control of their bodies and minds, fostering a sense of agency and self-efficacy. The discipline and determination required for physical exercise translate into other areas of their lives, enabling them to face adversity with strength and resilience.

Physical exercise plays a crucial role in the healing and recovery journey of teenagers facing trauma in the digital age. Through regular physical activity, teenagers can establish a strong mind-body connection, reduce stress, regulate emotions, enhance self-esteem, and foster resilience. Whether through cardiovascular workouts, strength training, yoga, or other forms of exercise, engaging in physical activity empowers teenagers to take control of their well-being, build self-confidence, and cultivate a positive body image. By incorporating physical exercise into their lives, teenagers can harness its transformative power to support their healing process, promote emotional wellness, and build resilience beyond trauma.

NOTES

Conclusion

Congratulations on completing your journey through "Unplugged! A Practical Guide to Managing Teenage Stress in the Digital Age." Throughout this book, we have explored proven techniques and strategies for promoting emotional wellness, achieving healthy habits, and building resilience in the face of the unique challenges faced by teenagers today. As your life coach, I want to take a moment to reflect on the valuable insights and transformational tools you have gained.

In **Chapter 1: <u>Stress</u> - Managing Stress in the Teenage Years and Beyond**, you have discovered the power of stillness and self-awareness. Through practices like meditation, journaling, and walking in nature, you have cultivated a sense of calm amidst the storms of life. These techniques have empowered you to navigate stress with grace, find inner peace, and unlock your full potential.

Chapter 2: <u>Academic Pressures</u> - Finding Balance - Managing Schoolwork and Personal Life has equipped you with essential skills to excel academically while maintaining a healthy balance. You have learned the art of effective time management, discovered study techniques tailored to your unique learning style, and embraced the importance of self-care. By prioritizing your well-being and establishing boundaries, you have embraced a harmonious integration of your academic and personal life.

In **Chapter 3:** <u>**Peer Pressure**</u> **- Navigating Healthy Relationships and Building Resilience**, you have unlocked the secrets to building authentic connections and fostering resilience. By harnessing the power of positive self-talk, seeking support from like-minded peers, and engaging in meaningful community service, you have cultivated a strong sense of self-worth, confidence, and the ability to make wise choices that align with your values.

Bullying, a prevalent issue in today's society, has been addressed in **Chapter 4: Bullying - Recognizing and Addressing Bullying: Empowering Individuals to Take Action**. You have learned invaluable strategies to build self-esteem, resolve conflicts peacefully, and develop social skills that promote respect and empathy. Armed with these tools, you have become a powerful advocate against bullying, creating a safe and inclusive environment for yourself and others.

The impact of social media on our lives cannot be ignored, and **Chapter 5:** <u>**Social Media**</u> **- Navigating the Digital Landscape for Healthy Engagement and Well-being** has guided you through the digital realm with wisdom. By setting boundaries, practicing mindful social media use, and managing your digital footprint, you have reclaimed control over your online experiences and established a healthy relationship with technology.

Chapter 6: <u>Political Climate</u> - Finding Common Ground: Building Bridges in a Divided Political Climate, has empowered you to navigate the complexities of the political landscape with grace and compassion. By embracing diverse perspectives, promoting media literacy, and fostering open-mindedness, you have become an agent of positive change, bridging divides and fostering understanding in a world often characterized by polarization.

Lastly, in **Chapter 7: <u>Trauma</u> - Understanding the Impact of Trauma: Building a Foundation for Recovery**, you have embarked on a healing journey. By seeking professional counseling, expressing yourself creatively, and engaging in physical exercise, you have confronted the impact of trauma head-on, paving the way for personal growth, resilience, and a brighter future.

As your life coach, I want to commend you for your commitment to personal growth and well-being. The tools and techniques you have acquired throughout this book will serve as lifelong companions on your journey to emotional wellness, healthy habits, and resilience. Remember, you possess the inner strength to overcome any challenge that comes your way.

Continue to nurture yourself, prioritize self-care, and surround yourself with positive influences. You are capable of achieving greatness and living a life filled with purpose, joy, and fulfillment. Embrace the lessons learned within these pages and let them guide you toward a future of endless possibilities.

Remember, you have the power to create the life you desire— one that is balanced, resilient, and filled with abundant happiness and success. You have taken a significant step towards managing teenage stress in the digital age and cultivating emotional well-being.

Always remember the importance of self-care and the power of self-reflection. Take time to nurture your mind, body, and spirit. Engage in activities that bring you joy, whether it's practicing mindfulness, pursuing creative outlets, or engaging in physical exercise. These practices will not only help you manage stress but also enhance your overall well-being. Building healthy habits is a lifelong journey, and this book has equipped you with practical strategies to achieve just that. Embrace the power of time management, study techniques, and self-care to find balance in your academic and personal life. By prioritizing your well-being, you will excel academically while maintaining a healthy and fulfilling lifestyle.

Navigating peer pressure can be challenging, but you now possess the tools to navigate healthy relationships and build resilience. Use positive self-talk to cultivate a strong sense of self-worth and inner strength. Seek support from like-minded peers who uplift and inspire you. Engaging in community service not only benefits others but also fosters personal growth and a sense of purpose.

Recognizing and addressing bullying is a crucial step in creating a safe and inclusive environment. By building self-esteem, resolving conflicts peacefully, and honing social skills, you are actively contributing to a culture of respect and empathy. Stand up against bullying, empower others, and be an advocate for positive change.

In the digital age, social media has become an integral part of our lives. However, it's essential to navigate this landscape mindfully. Set boundaries that protect your well-being and allow you to maintain a healthy relationship with technology. Manage your digital footprint to cultivate a positive online presence and protect your privacy. By using social media consciously, you can foster healthy engagement and well-being.

The current political climate can be divisive, but you have the power to build bridges and promote understanding. Embrace diverse perspectives, promote media literacy, and foster open-mindedness. By seeking common ground and engaging in constructive dialogue, you can contribute to a more harmonious and inclusive society.

Understanding the impact of trauma is crucial for building a foundation for recovery. Seek professional counseling to process and heal from traumatic experiences. Embrace creative expression as a means of self-discovery and healing. Engage in physical exercise to nurture your body and release emotional tension. Through these practices, you can embark on a journey of healing, resilience, and personal growth.

As you conclude your exploration of "Unplugged! A Practical Guide to Managing Teenage Stress in the Digital Age," remember that the journey doesn't end here. Continue to apply these proven techniques, strategies, and insights in your daily life. Embrace challenges as opportunities for growth and always prioritize your well-being and happiness.
You are not alone on this journey. Reach out to your support network—family, friends, mentors, and professionals—who are there to guide and uplift you. Remember, you possess the strength and resilience to overcome any obstacle that comes your way.

May this book serve as a constant source of inspiration, guidance, and empowerment. Embrace the path of emotional wellness, healthy habits, and building resilience, and watch yourself flourish into the remarkable individual you are destined to be.

Wishing you a life filled with joy, love, and success as you navigate the teenage years and beyond. You have the power to create a bright and fulfilling future. Unplug from stress, embrace your inner strength, and thrive in the digital age. Your journey starts now.

NOTES

Bibliography

Chapter 1. <u>Stress</u>
Managing Stress in the Teenage Years and Beyond

Managing Stress:

- McGonigal, Kelly. "The Upside of Stress: Why Stress Is Good for You, and How to Get Good at It." Avery, 2016.

- Lazarus, Richard S., and Folkman, Susan. "Stress, Appraisal, and Coping." Springer Publishing Company, 1984.

- Kabat-Zinn, Jon. "Full Catastrophe Living: Using the Wisdom of Your Body and Mind to Face Stress, Pain, and Illness." Delta, 1990.

- Chodron, Pema. "When Things Fall Apart: Heart Advice for Difficult Times." Shambhala Publications, 2000.

- Siebert, Al. "The Resiliency Advantage: Master Change, Thrive Under Pressure, and Bounce Back from Setbacks." Berrett-Koehler Publishers, 2005.

Meditation:

- Kabat-Zinn, Jon. "Wherever You Go, There You Are: Mindfulness Meditation in Everyday Life." Hachette Books, 1994.

- Salzberg, Sharon. "Real Happiness: The Power of Meditation: A 28-Day Program." Workman Publishing Company, 2010.

- Siegel, Daniel J. "Aware: The Science and Practice of Presence." TarcherPerigee, 2018.

- Ricard, Matthieu. "Happiness: A Guide to Developing

Life's Most Important Skill." Little, Brown and Company, 2007.

- McGonigal, Kelly. "The Willpower Instinct: How Self-Control Works, Why It Matters, and What You Can Do to Get More of It." Avery, 2012.

Journaling:

- Pennebaker, James W. "Opening Up: The Healing Power of Expressing Emotions." The Guilford Press, 1997.

- Ullrich, Philip M. "Journaling Power: How to Create the Happy, Healthy Life You Want to Live." Loving Healing Press, 2014.

- Adams, Kathleen. "Journal to the Self: Twenty-Two Paths to Personal Growth." Grand Central Publishing, 1990.

- Piver, Susan. "The New Book of Whole Grains: More than 200 Recipes featuring Whole Grains." Harvard Common Press, 2007.

- Murray, Laura. "The Artist's Way: A Spiritual Path to Higher Creativity." TarcherPerigee, 2002.

Walking in Nature:

- Louv, Richard. "Last Child in the Woods: Saving Our Children from Nature-Deficit Disorder." Algonquin Books, 2005.

- Ratey, John J. "Spark: The Revolutionary New Science of Exercise and the Brain." Little, Brown and Company, 2008.

- Thoreau, Henry David. "Walden." Princeton University Press, 2004.

- Mitchell, Richard. "Ponder on This: A Compilation." Lucis Publishing Company, 2003.

- Davis, Carolyn M. "Walking the Talk: Getting Fit with Faith." W Publishing Group, 2007.

Chapter 02. <u>Academic Pressures</u>
Finding Balance - Managing Schoolwork and Personal Life

Time Management:

- Covey, Stephen R. The 7 Habits of Highly Effective Teens. Fireside, 2014.

- Lakein, Alan. How to Get Control of Your Time and Your Life. Penguin Books, 1996.

- Tracy, Brian. Eat That Frog!: 21 Great Ways to Stop Procrastinating and Get More Done in Less Time. Berrett-Koehler Publishers, 2017.

- Vanderkam, Laura. Off the Clock: Feel Less Busy While Getting More Done. Penguin Books, 2019.

- Morgenstern, Julie. Time Management from the Inside Out: The Foolproof System for Taking Control of Your Schedule and Your Life. Henry Holt and Company, 2004.

- Egan, Mark. "The Power of Time Management." Psychology Today, 15 Sept. 2019, www.psychologytoday.com/us/blog/beyond-pleasure-and-pain/201909/the-power-time-management.

- Wiethoff, Alexandra, and Julia Hagen. "Time Management for Teens." The Harvard Crimson, 23 Nov. 2020, www.thecrimson.com/article/2020/11/23/time-management-teens/.

Study Techniques:

- Britton, B. K., & Tesser, A. (1991). Effects of time-management practices on college grades. Journal of Educational Psychology, 83(3), 405-410.

- Buzan, T. (2010). The mind map book: Unlock your creativity, boost your memory, change your life. BBC Active.

- Johnson, D. W., Johnson, R. T., & Smith, K. A. (2014). Cooperative learning: Improving university instruction by basing practice on validated theory. Journal on Excellence in College Teaching, 25(4), 85-118.

- Roediger, H. L., & Butler, A. C. (2011). The critical role of retrieval practice in long-term retention. Trends in Cognitive Sciences, 15(1), 20-27.

- Willis, J., & Farmer, R. (2020). Reading for Understanding: How Reading Apprenticeship Improves Disciplinary Learning in Secondary and College Classrooms (3rd ed.). John Wiley & Sons.

Self-Care:

- Carskadon, M. A., Acebo, C., & Jenni, O. G. (2006). Regulation of adolescent sleep: implications for behavior. Annals of the New York Academy of Sciences, 1021(1), 276-291.

- Dunning, D. L., Griffiths, K., Kuyken, W., Crane, C. (2019). Fostering Mindfulness in Parents, Carers, and Teachers: A Systematic Review and Meta-Analysis of Mindfulness-Based Interventions. Mindfulness, 10(5), 819-837.

- Mandolesi, L., Polverino, A., Montuori, S., Foti, F., Ferraioli, G., Sorrentino, P., ... & Sorrentino, G. (2018). Effects of Physical Exercise on Cognitive Functioning and Wellbeing: Biological and Psychological Benefits. Frontiers in

Psychology, 9, 509.

- National Sleep Foundation. (n.d.). Sleep Hygiene. Retrieved from https://www.sleepfoundation.org/sleep-hygiene

- US Department of Health and Human Services. (2019). Move Your Way: Physical Activity Guidelines for Americans. Retrieved from https://health.gov/sites/default/files/2019-09/Physical_Activity_Guidelines_2nd_edition.pdf

Chapter 3. Peer Pressure
Navigating Healthy Relationships and Building Resilience

Positive Self-Talk:

- Burns, D. D. (2009). Feeling Good: The New Mood Therapy. Harper.

- Chmitorz, A., Kunzler, A., Helmreich, I., Tüscher, O., & Kalisch, R. (2018). The influence of self-compassion on emotional well-being: A systematic review. Journal of Research in Personality, 74, 92-108.

- Leyfer, O. T., Ruberg, J. L., & Woodruff-Borden, J. (2006). Examination of the utility of the Beck Anxiety Inventory and its factors as a screener for anxiety disorders. Journal of Anxiety Disorders, 20(4), 444-458.

- McLeod, S. (2020). Self-Confidence. Simply Psychology. Retrieved from https://www.simplypsychology.org/self-confidence.html

- Sirois, F. M., & Wood, A. M. (2017). Gratitude uniquely predicts lower depression in chronic illness populations: A longitudinal study of inflammatory bowel disease and arthritis. Health Psychology, 36(2), 122-132.

Peer Support:

- Baker, C. N., & Daniels, C. R. (2019). Peer support arrangements: A review of the literature. Journal of Positive Behavior Interventions, 21(4), 213-226.

- Brown, B. B., & Larson, J. (2009). Peer relationships in adolescence. Handbook of Adolescent Psychology, 3, 74-103.

- Hamm, J. V. (2015). Peer relationships and adjustment at school. In Handbook of Peer Interactions, Relationships, and Groups (2nd ed., pp. 345-365). Guilford Press.

- Hurd, N. M., Zimmerman, M. A., & Xue, Y. (2010). Negative adult influences and the protective effects of role models: A study with urban adolescents. Journal of Youth and Adolescence, 39(7), 820-833.

- Scales, P. C., & Leffert, N. (2004). Developmental assets: A synthesis of the scientific research on adolescent development (2nd ed.). Search Institute.

Community Service:

- Clary, E. G., Snyder, M., Ridge, R. D., Copeland, J., Stukas, A. A., Haugen, J., & Miene, P. (1998). Understanding and assessing the motivations of volunteers: A functional approach. Journal of Personality and Social Psychology, 74(6), 1516-1530.

- Dávid-Barrett, T., & Dunbar, R. I. (2017). Bipedality and hair loss in human evolution revisited: The impact of altitude and activity scheduling. Journal of Human Evolution, 111, 14-19.

- Eom, K., Cupchik, G. C., & Byun, K. (2019). Understanding the relationships among leisure motivation, leisure satisfaction, and subjective well-being for adults with chronic illness. Journal of Leisure Research, 51(3), 215-229.

- Musick, M. A., & Wilson, J. (2003). Volunteering and depression: The role of psychological and social resources in different age groups. Social Science & Medicine, 56(2), 259-269.

- Stukas, A. A., Snyder, M., & Clary, E. G. (2016). The effects of "mandatory volunteerism" on intentions to volunteer. Psychological

Chapter 4. Bullying
Recognizing and Addressing Bullying: Empowering Individuals to Take Action

Building Self-Esteem:

- Neff, K. D. (2011). Self-compassion: Stop beating yourself up and leave insecurity behind. HarperCollins.

- McKay, M., & Fanning, P. (2016). Self-esteem: A proven program of cognitive techniques for assessing, improving, and maintaining your self-esteem. New Harbinger Publications.

- Crocker, J., & Park, L. E. (2004). The costly pursuit of self-esteem. Psychological Bulletin, 130(3), 392-414.

Conflict Resolution:

- Fisher, R., Ury, W., & Patton, B. (2011). Getting to yes: Negotiating agreement without giving in. Penguin.

- Deutsch, M., & Coleman, P. T. (Eds.). (2006). The handbook of conflict resolution: Theory and practice. Jossey-Bass.

- Folger, J. P., Poole, M. S., & Stutman, R. K. (2013). Working through conflict: Strategies for relationships, groups, and organizations. Pearson.

Social Skills Training:

- Gresham, F. M., & Elliott, S. N. (2008). Social skills improvement system: Rating scales manual. Pearson.

- Bellack, A. S., Hersen, M., & Turner, S. M. (Eds.). (2008). Handbook of social functioning in schizophrenia. Elsevier.

- Matson, J. L., & Matson, M. L. (Eds.). (2011). Social skills: Advances in research and practice. Springer Science & Business Media.

Chapter 5: Social Media
Navigating the Digital Landscape for Healthy Engagement and Well-being

Setting Boundaries:

- Bono, K., & Itano, N. (2019). "The relationship between social media boundaries and life satisfaction." Computers in Human Behavior, 95, 74-81.

- Crisp, D. A., & Turner, N. E. (2019). "The role of boundaries in managing social media use: perspectives of early adolescents and their parents." Journal of Children and Media, 13(2), 219-235.

- Evans, S., Pearce, K., Vitak, J., & Treem, J. W. (2017). "Explicating affordances: A conceptual framework for understanding affordances in communication research." Journal of Computer-Mediated Communication, 22(1), 35-52.

Mindful Social Media Use:

- Chou, H. G., & Edge, N. (2012). "They are happier and having better lives than I am": The impact of using Facebook on perceptions of others' lives. Cyberpsychology, Behavior, and Social Networking, 15(2), 117-121.

- Rosen, L. D., Whaling, K., Carrier, L. M., Cheever, N. A., & Rokkum, J. (2013). "The media and technology usage and attitudes scale: An empirical investigation." Computers in Human Behavior, 29(6), 2501-2511.

- Turel, O., & Qahri-Saremi, H. (2016). "Problematic use of social networking sites: Antecedents and consequence from a dual-system theory perspective." Journal of Management Information Systems, 33(4), 1087-1116.

Digital Footprint Management:

- Baumeister, R. F., & Leary, M. R. (1995). "The need to belong: Desire for interpersonal attachments as a fundamental human motivation." Psychological Bulletin, 117(3), 497-529.

- Boyd, D. (2014). "It's complicated: The social lives of networked teens." Yale University Press.

- Boyd, D., & Marwick, A. E. (2011). "Social privacy in networked publics: Teens' attitudes, practices, and strategies." Paper presented at the Oxford Internet Institute's "A Decade in Internet Time: Symposium on the Dynamics of the Internet and Society."

Chapter 6: Political Climate
Finding Common Ground: Building Bridges in a Divided Political Climate

Provide Diverse Perspectives:

- Sunstein, C. R. (2017). #Republic: Divided Democracy in the Age of Social Media. Princeton University Press.

- Phillips, K. (2016). The Politics of Resentment: Rural Consciousness in Wisconsin and the Rise of Scott Walker. University of Chicago Press.

- Hochschild, A. R. (2016). Strangers in Their Own Land: Anger and Mourning on the American Right. The New Press.

- Lippmann, W. (2013). Public Opinion. Routledge.

Promote Media Literacy:

- Hobbs, R. (2017). Create to Learn: Introduction to Digital Literacy. John Wiley & Sons.

- Jenkins, H., Clinton, K., Purushotma, R., Robison, A. J., & Weigel, M. (2009).

- Confronting the Challenges of Participatory Culture: Media Education for the 21st Century. The MIT Press.

- Livingstone, S. (2021). The Class: Living and Learning in the Digital Age. New York University Press.

- Buckingham, D. (2019). Media Education: Literacy, Learning, and Contemporary Culture. John Wiley & Sons.

Foster Open-Mindedness:

- Haidt, J. (2013). The Righteous Mind: Why Good People Are Divided by Politics and Religion. Vintage.

- Westen, D. (2008). The Political Brain: The Role of Emotion in Deciding the Fate of the Nation. PublicAffairs.
- Nussbaum, M. C. (2016). Anger and Forgiveness: Resentment, Generosity, Justice. Oxford University Press.

- Sen, A. (2006). Identity and Violence: The Illusion of Destiny. W. W. Norton & Company.

Chapter 7: <u>Trauma</u>
Understanding the Impact of Trauma:
Building a Foundation for Recovery

Professional Counseling:

- Courtois, C. A., & Ford, J. D. (Eds.). (2013). Treating complex traumatic stress disorders: An evidence-based guide. Guilford Press.

- Herman, J. L. (1997). Trauma and recovery: The aftermath of violence—from domestic abuse to political terror. Basic Books.

- Resick, P. A., Bovin, M. J., Calloway, A. L., Dick, A. M., King, M. W., Mitchell, K. S., ... & Wolf, E. J. (2016). A critical evaluation of the complex PTSD literature: Implications for DSM-5. Journal of Traumatic Stress, 29(5), 399-408.

Creative Expression:

- Malchiodi, C. A. (Ed.). (2012). Handbook of art therapy. Guilford Press.

- Stuckey, H. L., & Nobel, J. (2010). The connection between art, healing, and public health: A review of current literature. American Journal of Public Health, 100(2), 254-263.

- van Lith, T., Fenstermacher, K., & Hammer, E. (2016). The effectiveness of expressive arts therapies to reduce trauma symptoms: A systematic review and meta-analysis. Psychotherapy Research, 26(2), 213-223.

Physical Exercise:

- Brown, R. P., & Gerbarg, P. L. (2005). Sudarshan Kriya Yogic breathing in the treatment of stress, anxiety, and depression: Part I-neurophysiologic model. The Journal of Alternative and Complementary Medicine, 11(1), 189-201.

- Gerber, M., & Kalak, N. (2016). Fitness and exercise as correlates of sleep complaints: Is it all in our minds? Medicine and Sport Science, 60, 66-74.

- Salmon, P. (2001). Effects of physical exercise on anxiety, depression, and sensitivity to stress: A unifying theory. Clinical Psychology Review, 21(1), 33-61.

Suggested Reading List

Chapter 1. <u>Stress</u>
Managing Stress in the Teenage Years and Beyond

- "The Stress Reduction Workbook for Teens: Mindfulness Skills to Help You Deal with Stress" by Gina M. Biegel

- "The Anxiety Workbook for Teens: Activities to Help You Deal with Anxiety and Worry" by Lisa M. Schab

- "Walking in This World: The Practical Art of Creativity" by Julia Cameron

Chapter 02. <u>Academic Pressures</u>
Finding Balance - Managing Schoolwork and Personal Life

- "The 7 Habits of Highly Effective Teens" by Sean Covey

- "How to Become a Straight-A Student: The Unconventional Strategies Real College Students Use to Score High While Studying Less" by Cal Newport

- "The Self-Care Solution: A Modern Mother's Must-Have Guide to Health and Well-being" by Julie Burton

Chapter 3. <u>Peer Pressure</u>
Navigating Healthy Relationships and Building Resilience

- "The Confidence Code for Girls: Taking Risks, Messing Up, and Becoming Your Amazingly Imperfect, Totally Powerful Self" by Katty Kay and Claire Shipman

- "Queen Bees and Wannabes: Helping Your Daughter Survive Cliques, Gossip, Boyfriends, and the New Realities of Girl World" by Rosalind Wiseman

- "The Power of Community: CrossFit and the Force of Human Connection" by CJ Martin

Chapter 4. Bullying
Recognizing and Addressing Bullying: Empowering Individuals to Take Action

- "Odd Girl Out: The Hidden Culture of Aggression in Girls" by Rachel Simmons

- "The Bully, the Bullied, and the Bystander: From Preschool to High School—How Parents and Teachers Can Help Break the Cycle" by Barbara Coloroso

- "Teaching Kids to Think: Raising Confident, Independent, and Thoughtful Children in an Age of Instant Gratification" by Darlene Sweetland and Ron Stolberg

Chapter 5: Social Media
Navigating the Digital Landscape for Healthy Engagement and Well-being

- "Digital Minimalism: Choosing a Focused Life in a Noisy World" by Cal Newport

- "The Art of Screen Time: How Your Family Can Balance Digital Media and Real Life" by Anya Kamenetz

- "So You've Been Publicly Shamed" by Jon Ronson

Chapter 6: Political Climate
Finding Common Ground: Building Bridges in a Divided Political Climate

- "I Think You're Wrong (But I'm Listening): A Guide to Graceful Disagreement" by Sarah Stewart Holland and Beth A. Silvers

- "The Righteous Mind: Why Good People Are Divided by Politics and Religion" by Jonathan Haidt

- "The Open Mind: Exploring the 6 Patterns of Natural Intelligence" by Dawna Markova

Chapter 7: <u>Trauma</u>
Understanding the Impact of Trauma:
Building a Foundation for Recovery

- "The Body Keeps the Score: Brain, Mind, and Body in the Healing of Trauma" by Bessel van der Kolk

- "Creative Interventions for Bereaved Children" by Liana Lowenstein

- "The Body Remembers: The Psychophysiology of Trauma and Trauma Treatment" by Babette Rothschild

NOTES

www.ingramcontent.com/pod-product-compliance
Lightning Source LLC
Chambersburg PA
CBHW060240030426
42335CB00014B/1547